HAL•LEONARD
GUITAR
PLAY·ALONG

alternative'90s

T0040775

Tracking, mixing, and mastering by
Jake Johnson & Bill Maynard at Paradyme Productions
All guitars by Doug Boduch
Bass by Tom McGirr
Drums by Scott Schroedl

ISBN-13: 978-0-634-07641-1
ISBN-10: 0-634-07641-8

Visit Hal Leonard Online at **www.halleonard.com**

HAL•LEONARD®
CORPORATION
7777 W. BLUEMOUND RD. P.O. BOX 13819 MILWAUKEE, WI 53213

Guitar Notation Legend

THE MUSICAL STAFF shows pitches and rhythms and is divided by bar lines into measures. Pitches are named after the first seven letters of the alphabet.

TABLATURE graphically represents the guitar fingerboard. Each horizontal line represents a string, and each number represents a fret.

4th string, 2nd fret   1st & 2nd strings open, played together   open D chord

---

HALF-STEP BEND: Strike the note and bend up 1/2 step.

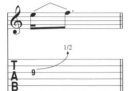

WHOLE-STEP BEND: Strike the note and bend up one step.

GRACE NOTE BEND: Strike the note and immediately bend up as indicated.

SLIGHT (MICROTONE) BEND: Strike the note and bend up 1/4 step.

BEND AND RELEASE: Strike the note and bend up as indicated, then release back to the original note. Only the first note is struck.

PRE-BEND: Bend the note as indicated, then strike it.

VIBRATO: The string is vibrated by rapidly bending and releasing the note with the fretting hand.

PALM MUTING: The note is partially muted by the pick hand lightly touching the string(s) just before the bridge.

HAMMER-ON: Strike the first (lower) note with one finger, then sound the higher note (on the same string) with another finger by fretting it without picking.

PULL-OFF: Place both fingers on the notes to be sounded. Strike the first note and without picking, pull the finger off to sound the second (lower) note.

LEGATO SLIDE: Strike the first note and then slide the same fret-hand finger up or down to the second note. The second note is not struck.

SHIFT SLIDE: Same as legato slide, except the second note is struck.

TRILL: Very rapidly alternate between the notes indicated by continuously hammering on and pulling off.

TAPPING: Hammer ("tap") the fret indicated with the pick-hand index or middle finger and pull off to the note fretted by the fret hand.

NATURAL HARMONIC: Strike the note while the fret-hand lightly touches the string directly over the fret indicated.

PINCH HARMONIC: The note is fretted normally and a harmonic is produced by adding the edge of the thumb or the tip of the index finger of the pick hand to the normal pick attack.

TREMOLO PICKING: The note is picked as rapidly and continuously as possible.

VIBRATO BAR DIVE AND RETURN: The pitch of the note or chord is dropped a specified number of steps (in rhythm), then returned to the original pitch.

VIBRATO BAR SCOOP: Depress the bar just before striking the note, then quickly release the bar.

VIBRATO BAR DIP: Strike the note and then immediately drop a specified number of steps, then release back to the original pitch.

Additional Musical Definitions

 (accent)
- Accentuate note (play it louder).

 (staccato)
- Play the note short.

D.S. al Coda
- Go back to the sign (%), then play until the measure marked "*To Coda*," then skip to the section labelled "**Coda**."

D.C. al Fine
- Go back to the beginning of the song and play until the measure marked "*Fine*" (end).

Fill
- Label used to identify a brief melodic figure which is to be inserted into the arrangement.

N.C.
- Harmony is implied.

- Repeat measures between signs.

- When a repeated section has different endings, play the first ending only the first time and the second ending only the second time.

HAL·LEONARD

GUITAR
PLAY·ALONG

alternative'90s

CONTENTS

Page	Title	Demo Track	Play-Along Track
4	Alive PEARL JAM	1	2
12	Been Caught Stealing JANE'S ADDICTION	3	4
18	Cherub Rock SMASHING PUMPKINS	5	6
38	Come as You Are NIRVANA	7	8
46	Give It Away RED HOT CHILI PEPPERS	9	10
56	No Excuses ALICE IN CHAINS	11	12
27	No Rain BLIND MELON	13	14
60	Santeria SUBLIME	15	16
	TUNING NOTES	17	

Alive

Music by Stone Gossard
Lyric by Eddie Vedder

Intro

Moderately slow Rock ♩ = 76

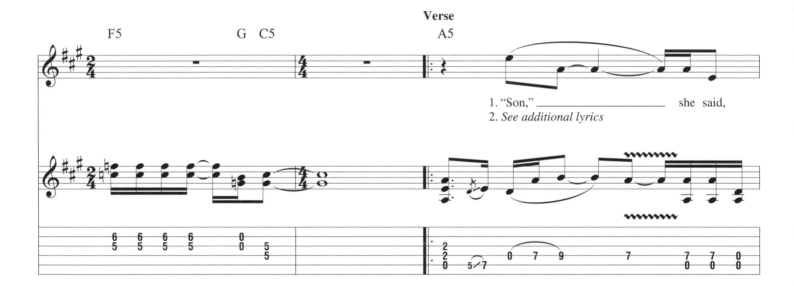

Verse

1. "Son," _____ she said,
2. *See additional lyrics*

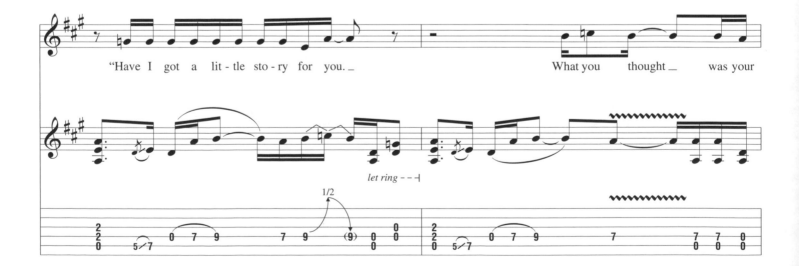

"Have I got a lit-tle sto-ry for you.___

What you thought ___ was your

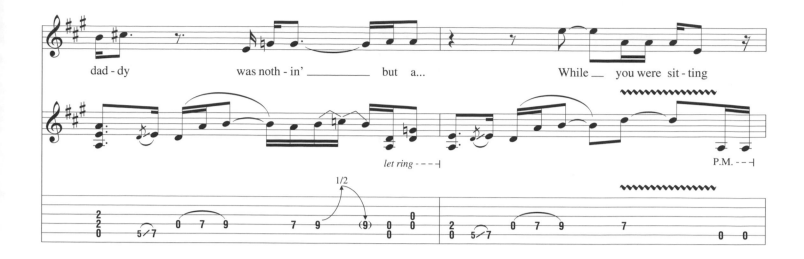

dad - dy was noth - in' _____ but a... While __ you were sit - ting

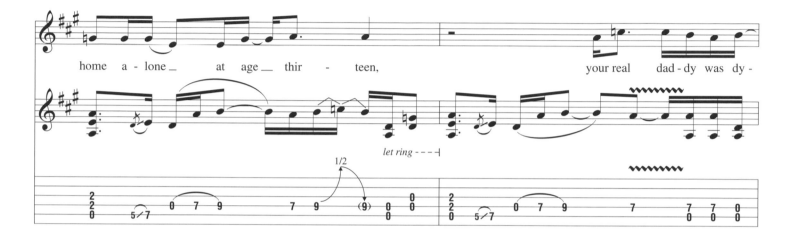

home a - lone __ at age __ thir - teen, your real dad - dy was dy -

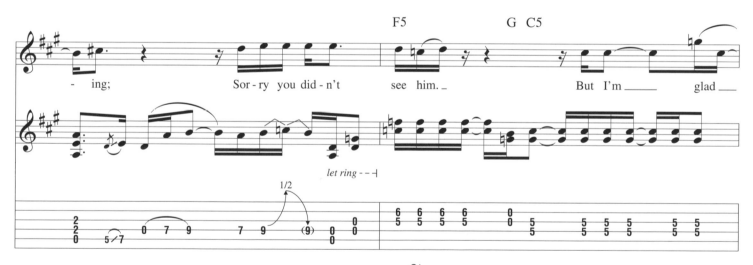

- ing; Sor - ry you did - n't see him. __ But I'm _____ glad _____

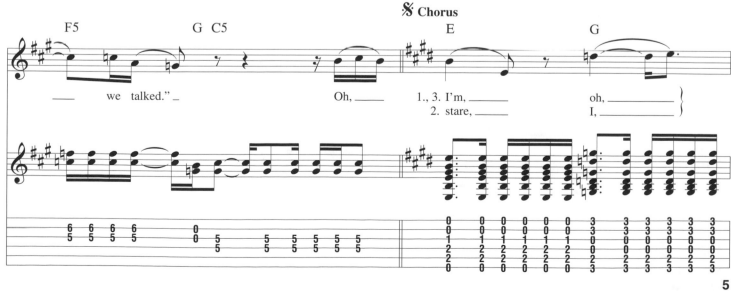

_____ we talked." _ Oh, _____ oh, _____

1., 3. I'm, _____
2. stare, _____ I, _____

𝄋 Chorus

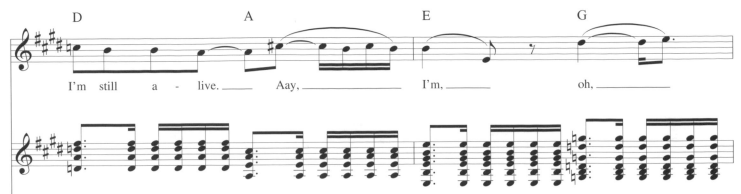

I'm still a - live.____ Aay,_____ I'm,_____ oh,____

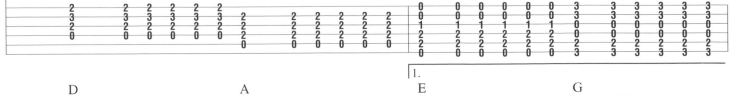

1.

I'm still a - live.____ Aay,_____ I'm,_____ oh,____

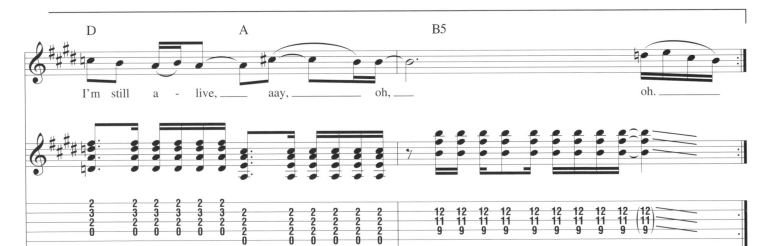

I'm still a - live,____ aay,_____ oh, ___ oh.____

2.

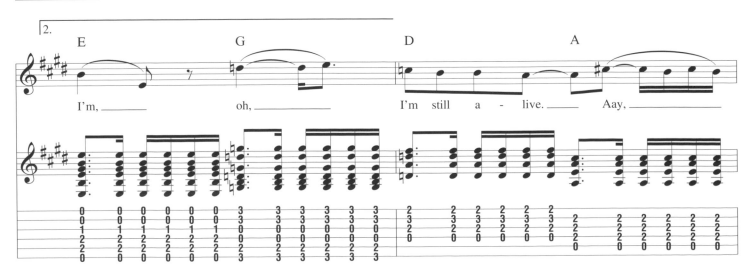

I'm,_____ oh,_____ I'm still a - live.____ Aay,____

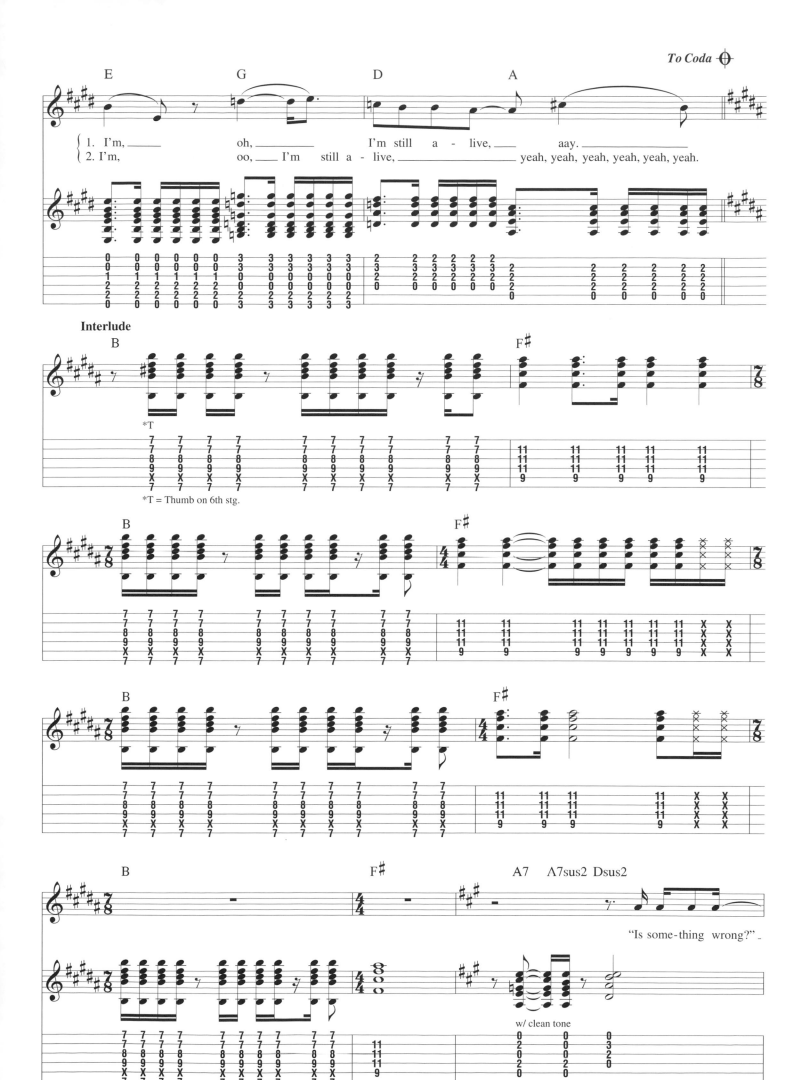

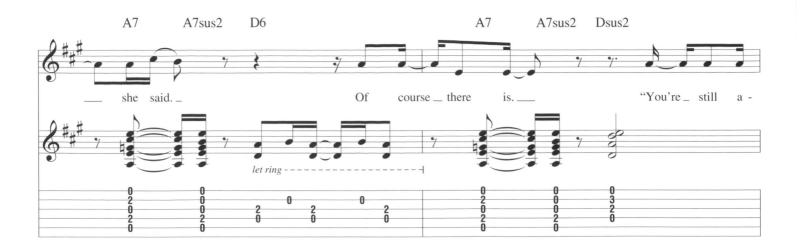

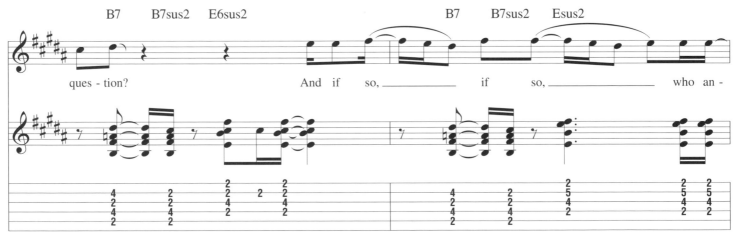

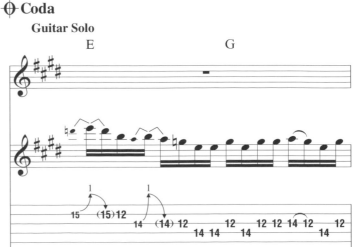

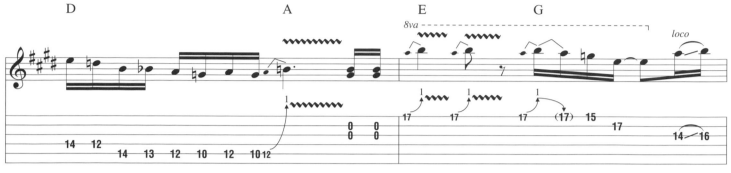

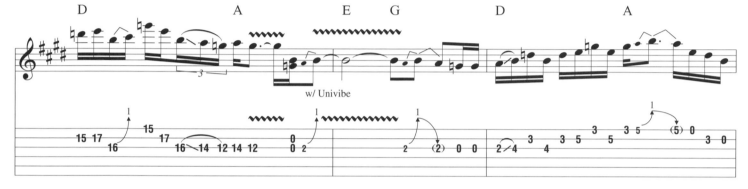

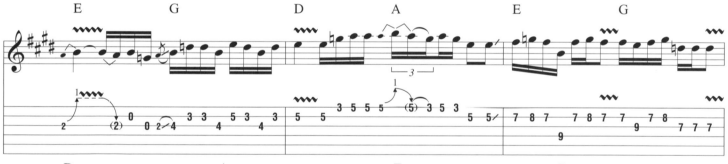

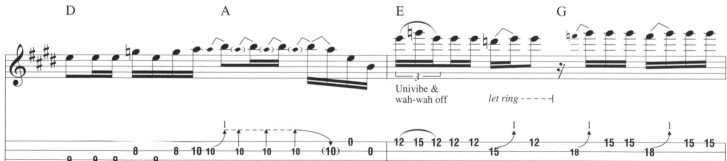

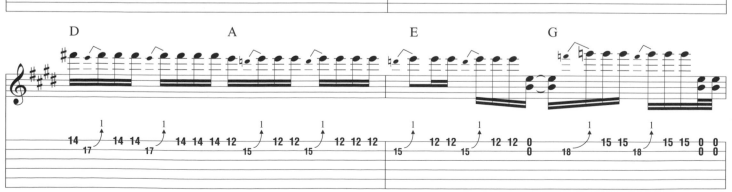

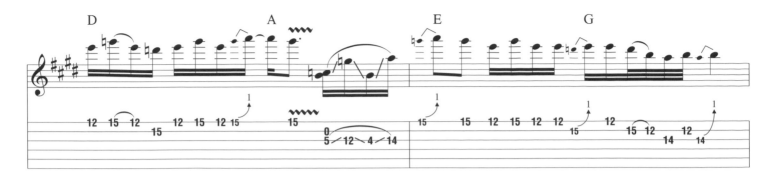

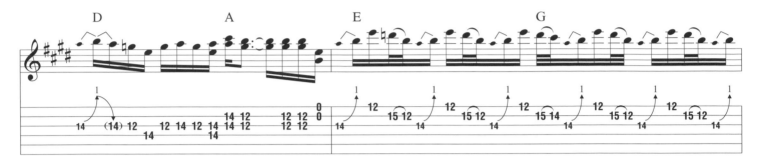

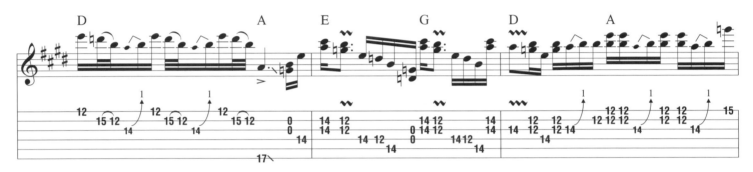

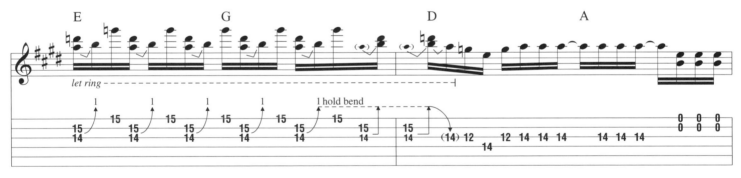

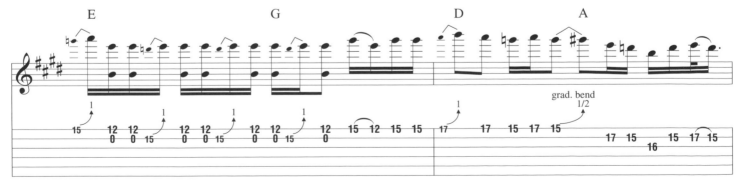

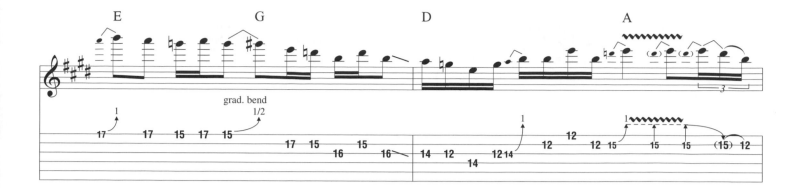

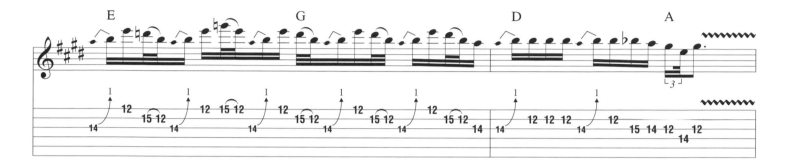

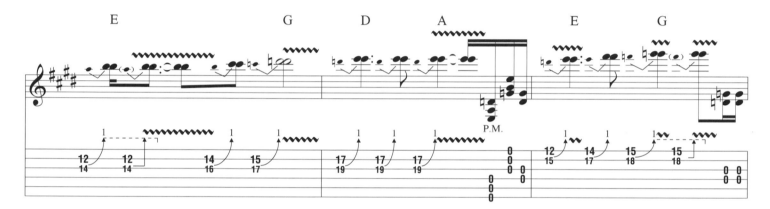

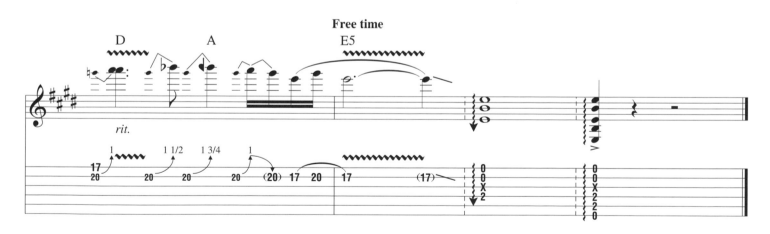

Additional Lyrics

2. While she walks slowly
   Across a young man's room,
   She said, "I'm ready for you."
   I can't remember anything to this very day,
   'Cept the love, the love.
   Oh, you know where, now I can see.

Been Caught Stealing

Written by Perry Farrell, Dave Navaro, Stephen Perkins and Eric Avery

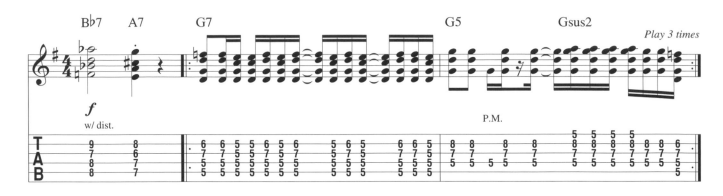

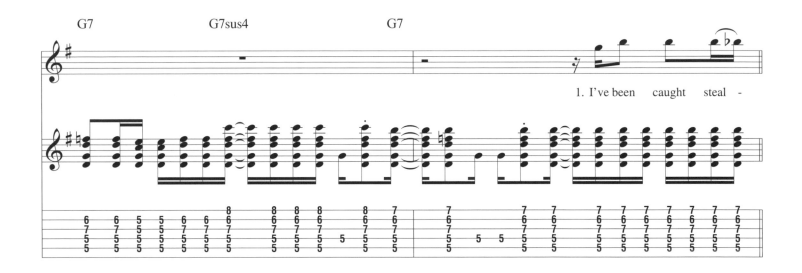

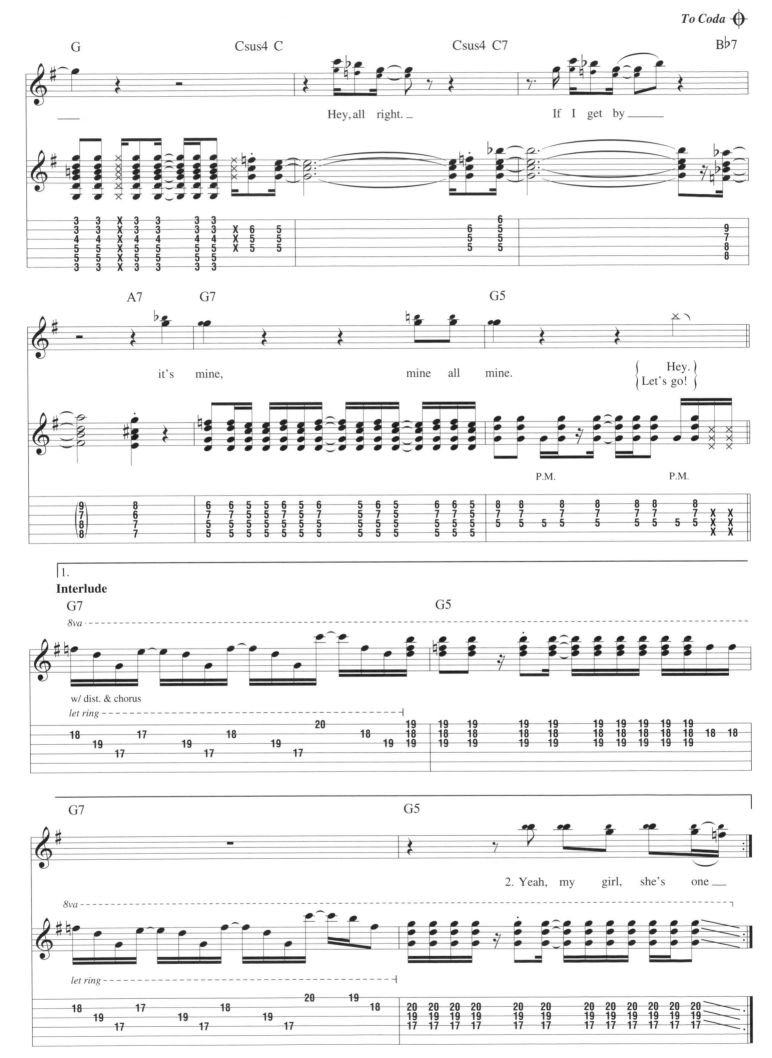

[2.

Guitar Solo

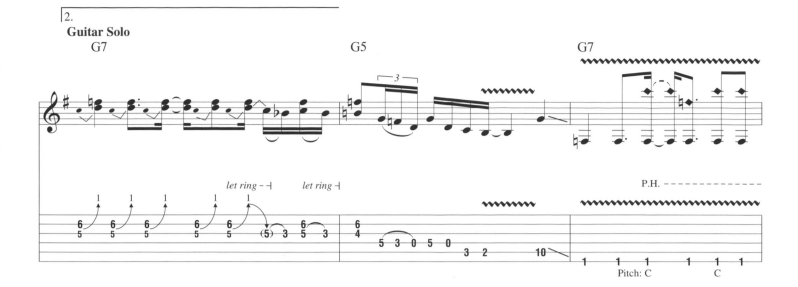

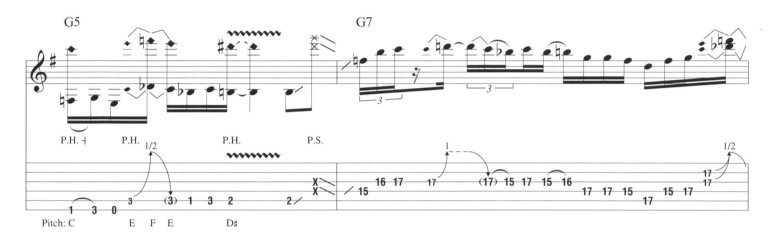

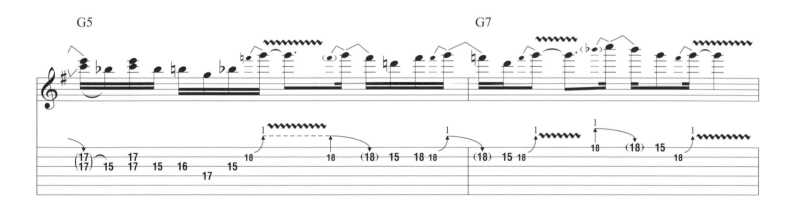

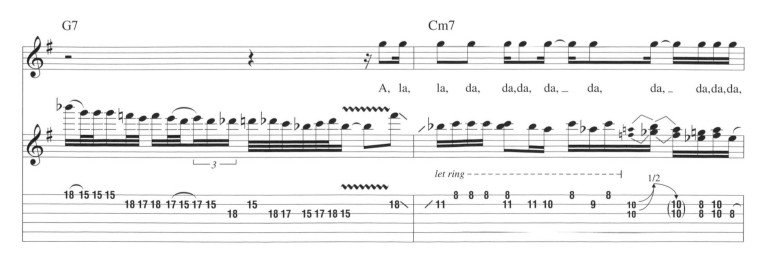

⊕ Coda

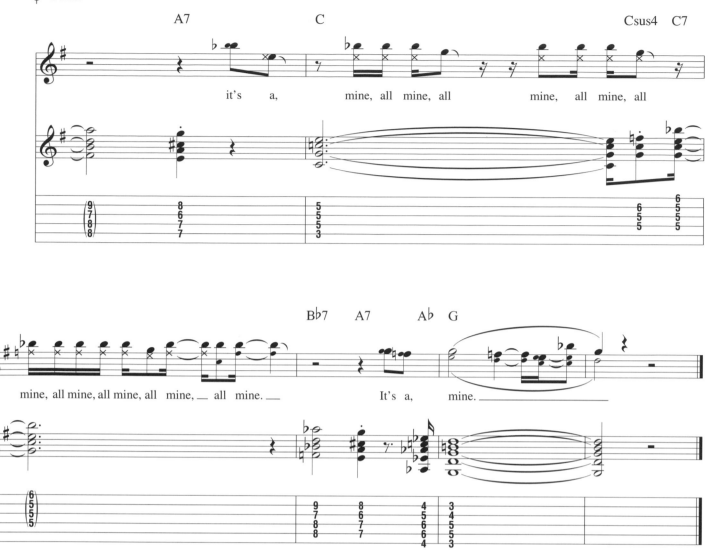

Additional Lyrics

2. Yeah, my girl, she's one too.
   She'll go and get her a skirt,
   Stick it under her shirt.
   She grabbed a razor for me.
   And she did it just like that
   When she wants something
   And she don't want to pay for it.
   She walk right through the door,
   Walk right through the door.
   Hey, all right. If I get by
   It's a mine, mine all mine. Let's go!

3. Sat around the pile, sat and laughed.
   Sat and laughed and waved 'em into the air.
   And we did it just like that
   When we want something
   And we don't want to pay for it.
   We walk right through the door,
   Walk right through the door.
   Hey, all right. If I get by...

Cherub Rock

Words and Music by Billy Corgan

Intro
Moderate Rock ♩ = 85

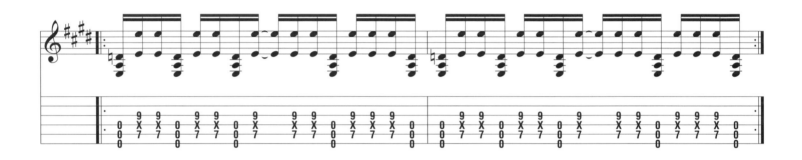

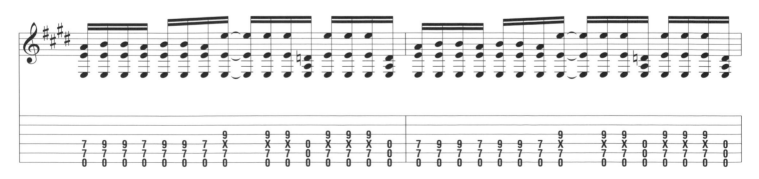

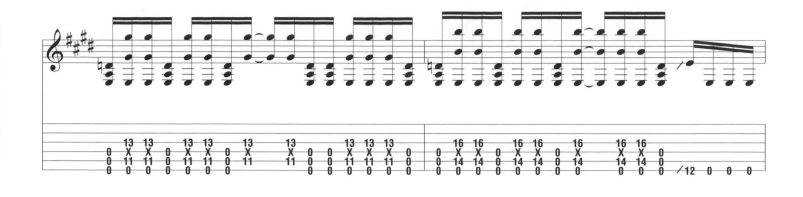

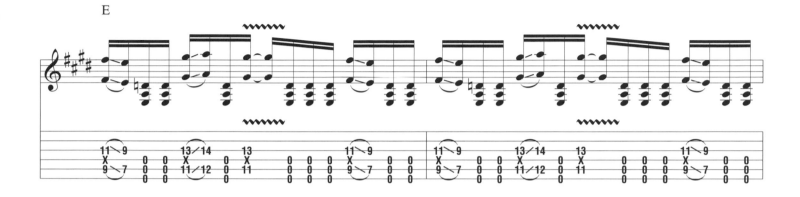

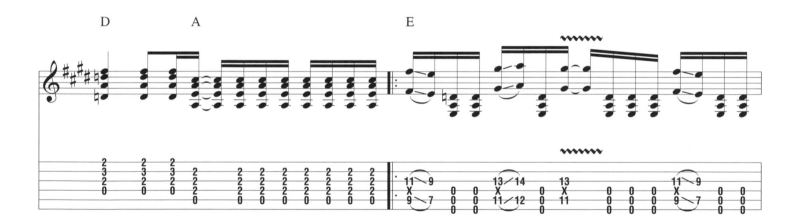

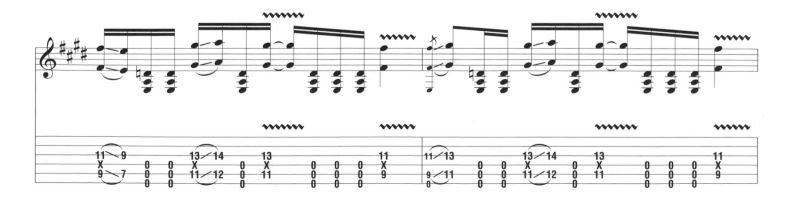

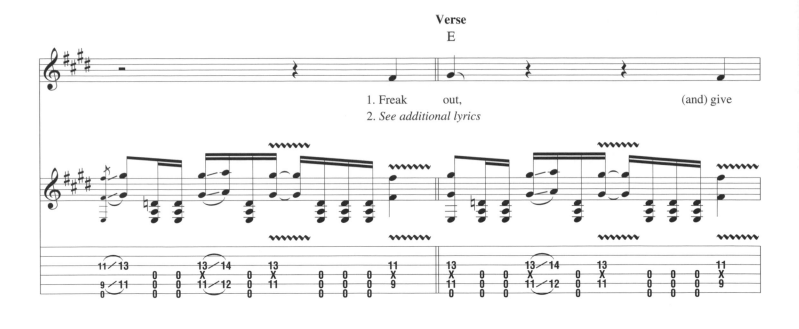

1. Freak out, (and) give
2. *See additional lyrics*

in, does-n't mat - ter what you be - lieve in.

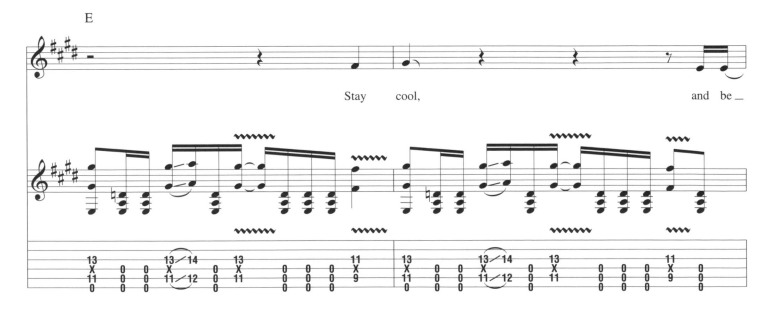

Stay cool, and be ___

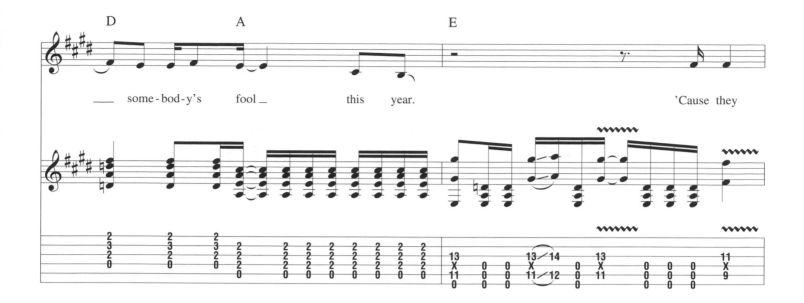

some-bod-y's fool _ this year. 'Cause they

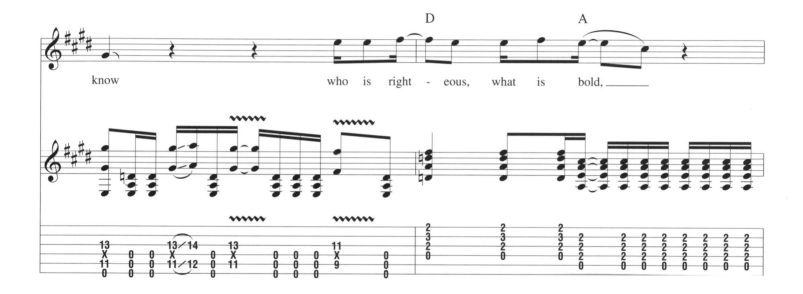

know who is right - eous, what is bold, _

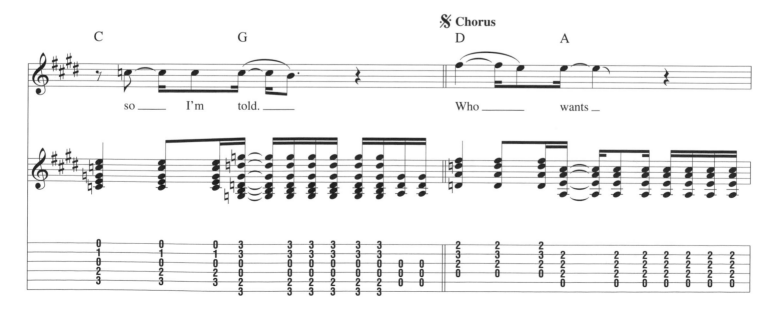

so _ I'm told. _ Who _ wants _

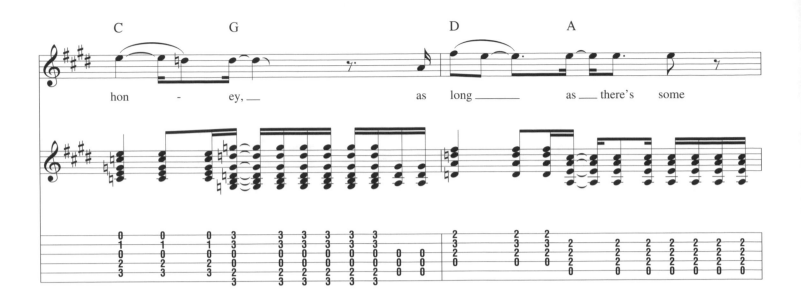

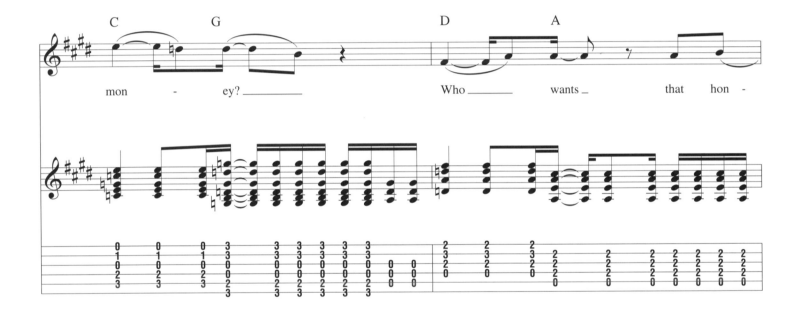

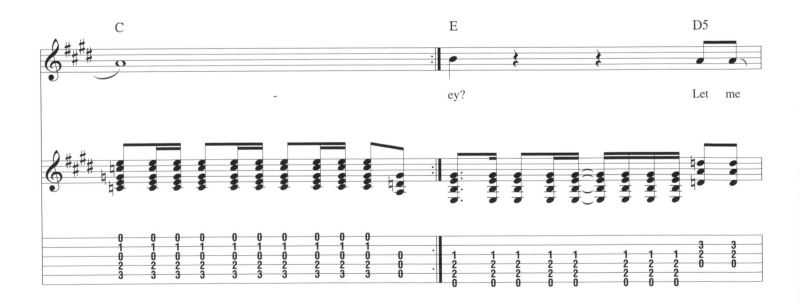

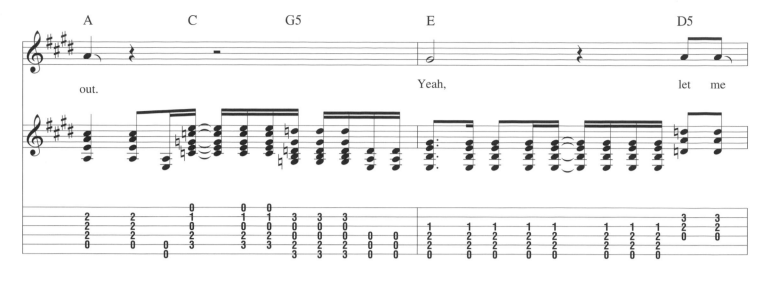

out.

Yeah,

let me

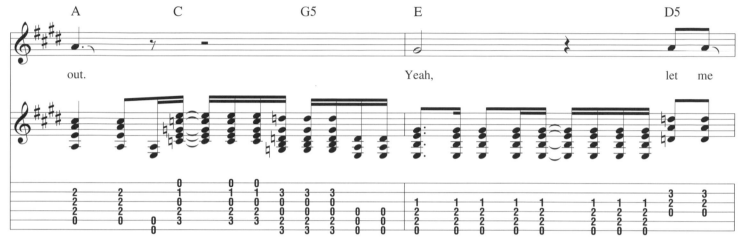

out.

Yeah,

let me

To Coda ⊕

out. ___

Yeah, ___

let me out! _____

Interlude

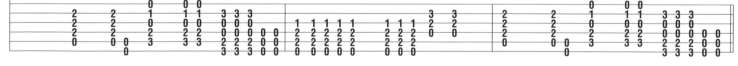

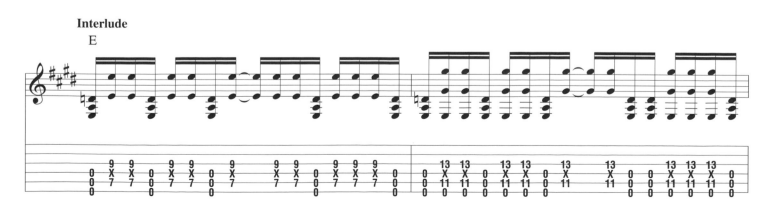

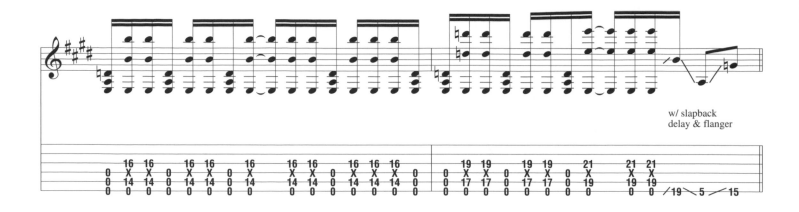

w/ slapback
delay & flanger

Guitar Solo

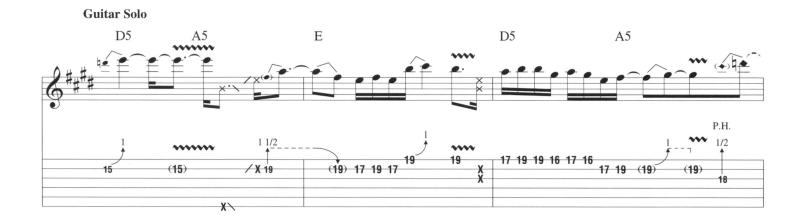

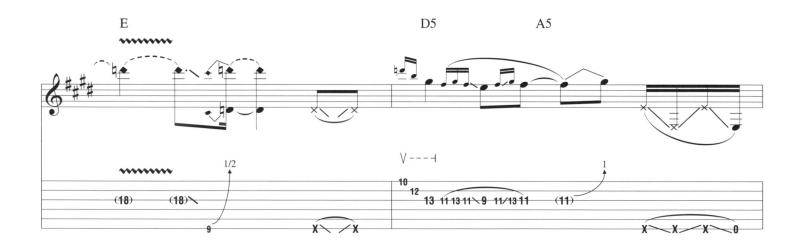

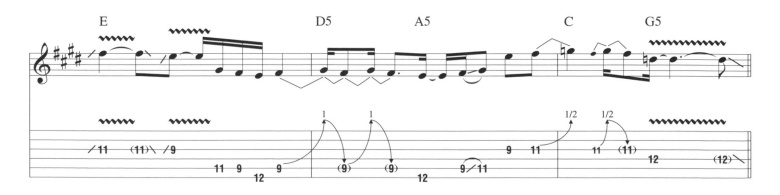

Bridge

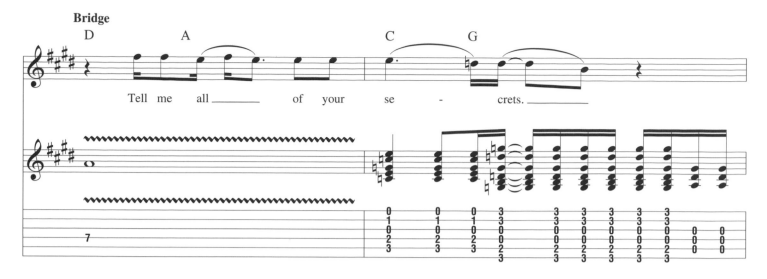

Tell me all _____ of your se - crets. _____

Can - not help _____ but be - lieve _____ this ___ is true. ___

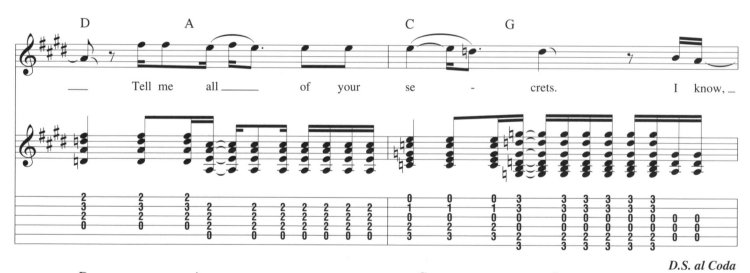

___ Tell me all _____ of your se - crets. I know, ___

D.S. al Coda

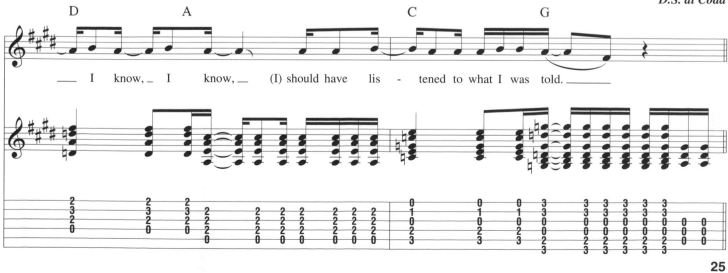

___ I know, __ I know, ___ (I) should have lis - tened to what I was told. _____

⊕ Coda

Outro

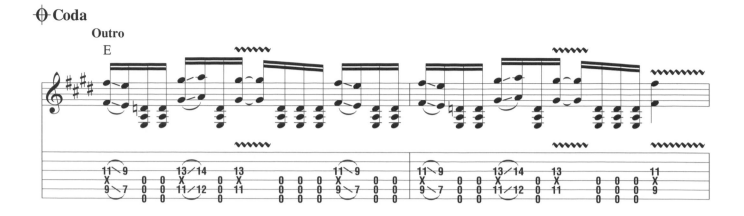

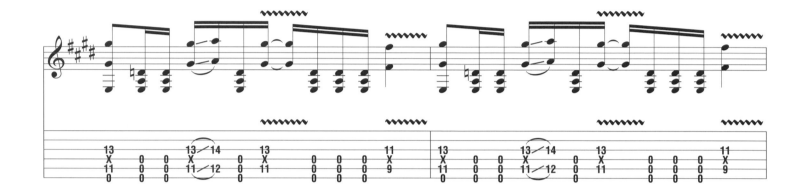

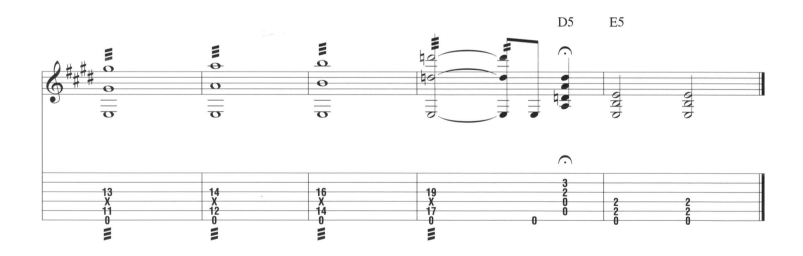

Additional Lyrics

2. Hipsters unite;
   Come align for the big fight to rock for you.
   But beware,
   All those angels with their wings glued on,
   'Cause deep down
   They are frightened and they're scared
   If you don't stare.

No Rain

Words and Music by Blind Melon

Intro
Moderately fast Rock ♩ = 160

mf
w/ clean tone & delay

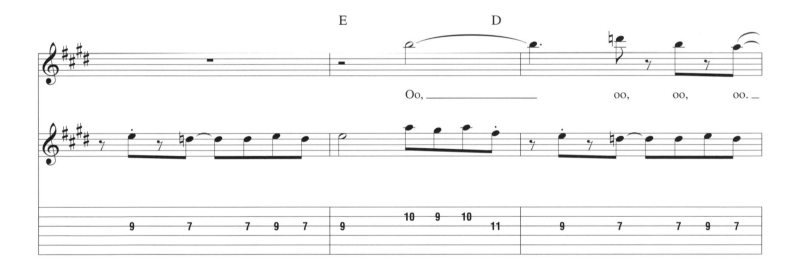

Oo,_____ oo, oo, oo.__

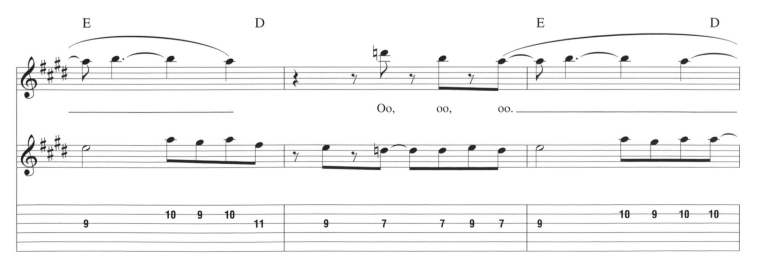

Oo, oo, oo.__

Verse

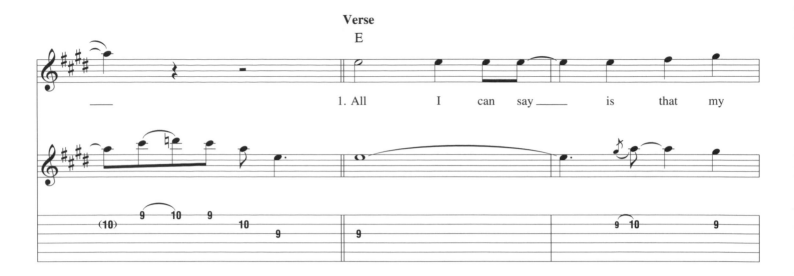

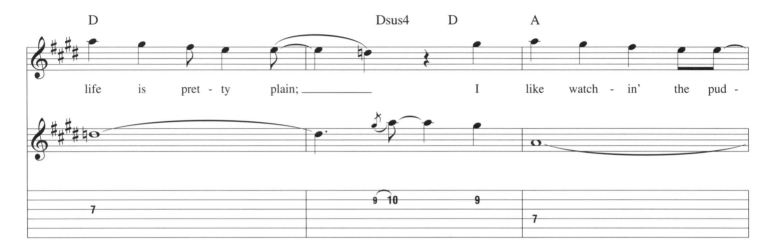

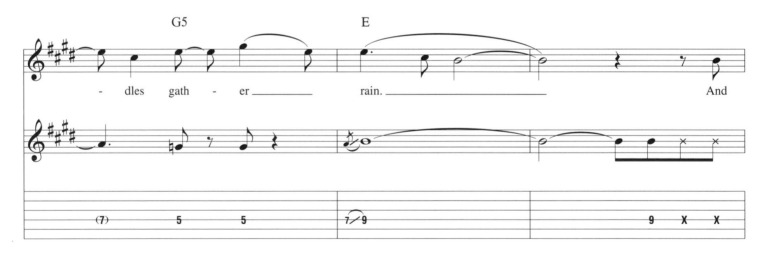

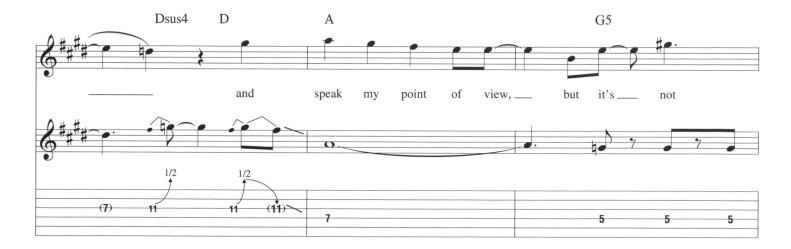

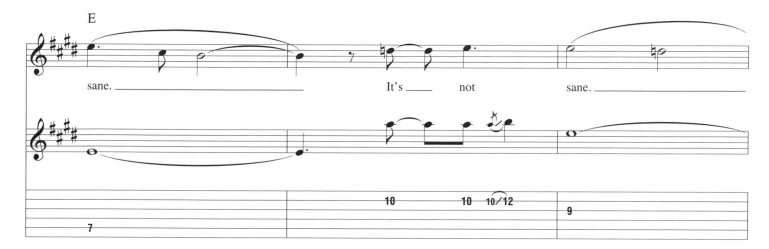

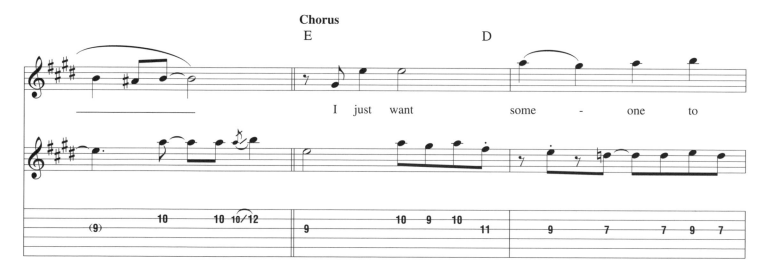

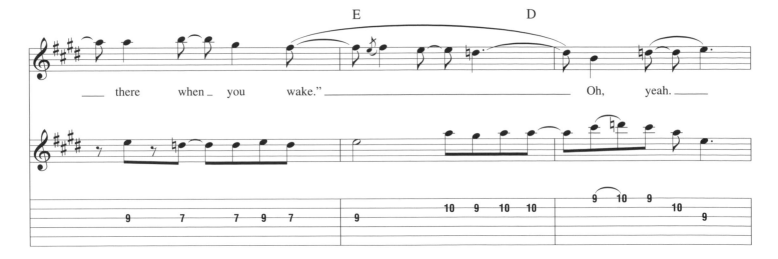

there when you wake." Oh, yeah.

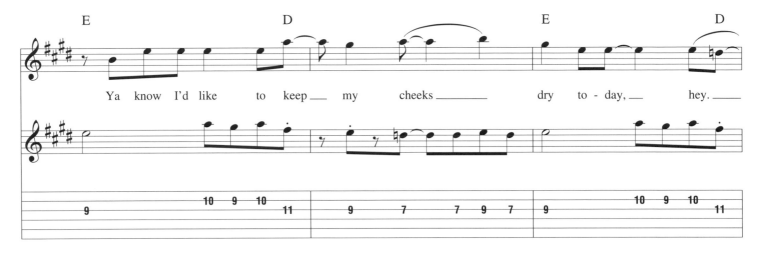

Ya know I'd like to keep my cheeks dry to - day, hey.

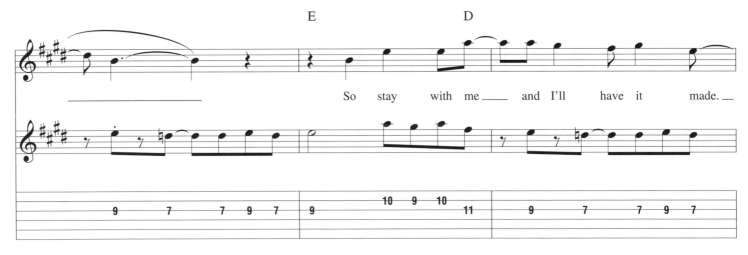

So stay with me and I'll have it made.

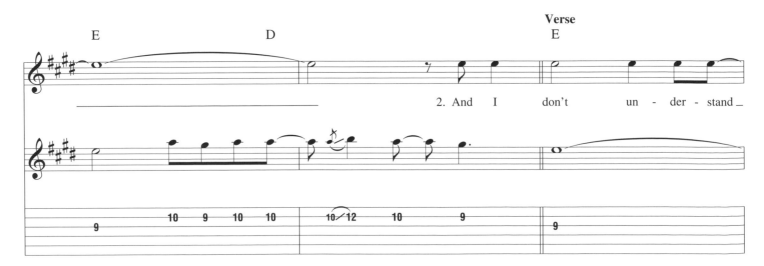

Verse

2. And I don't un - der - stand

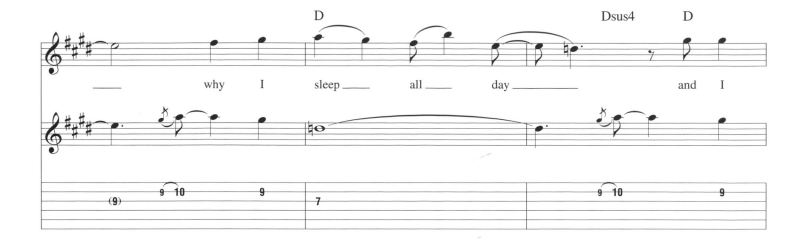

why I sleep ___ all ___ day ___ and I

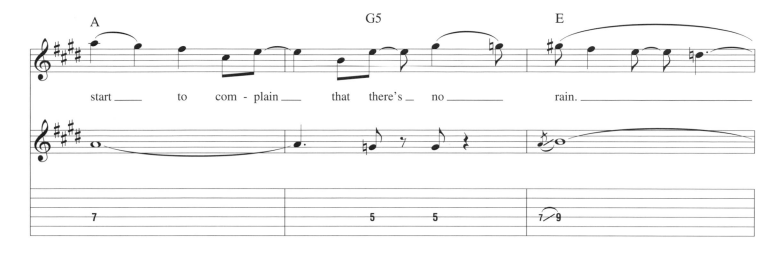

start ___ to com - plain ___ that there's ___ no ___ rain. ___

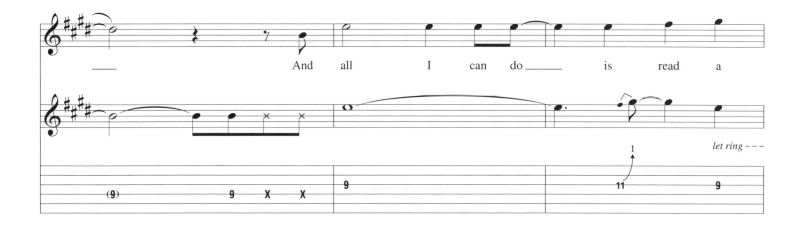

___ And all I can do ___ is read a

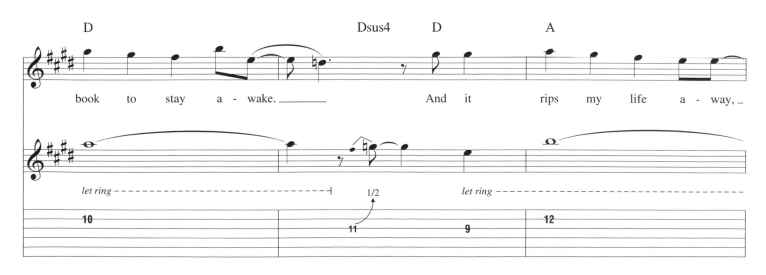

book to stay a - wake. ___ And it rips my life a - way, ___

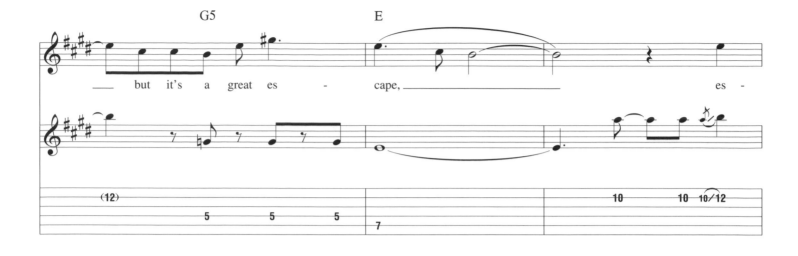

but it's a great es - cape, _____ es -

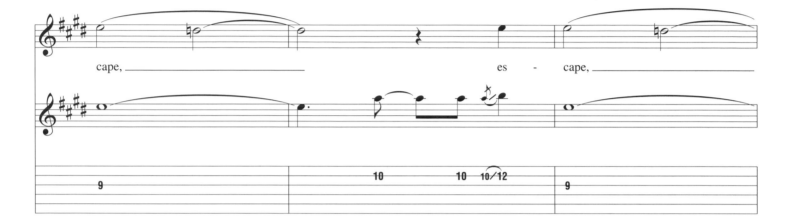

cape, _____ es - cape, _____

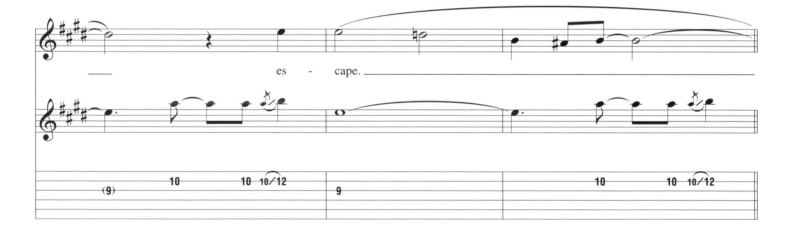

es - cape. _____

Guitar Solo

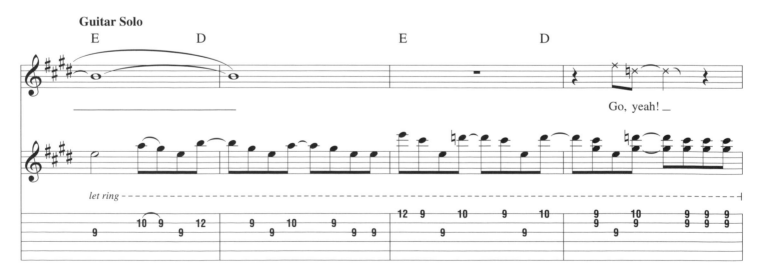

Go, yeah! _

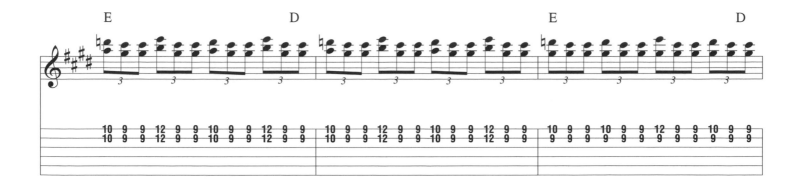

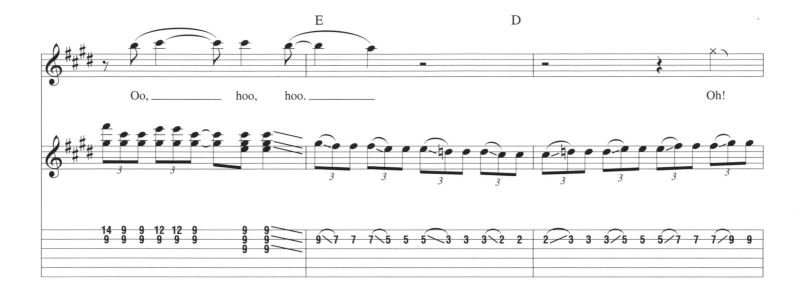

Oo, _____ hoo, hoo. _____ Oh!

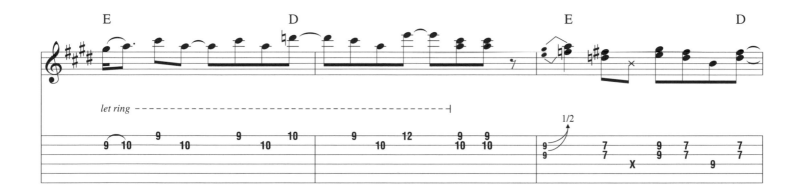

Verse

3. All I can say _____ is that my life is pret-ty plain. _____ You don't like my point of view; _____ you think that I'm in - sane. It's _____ not sane. _____ It's _____ not sane. _____

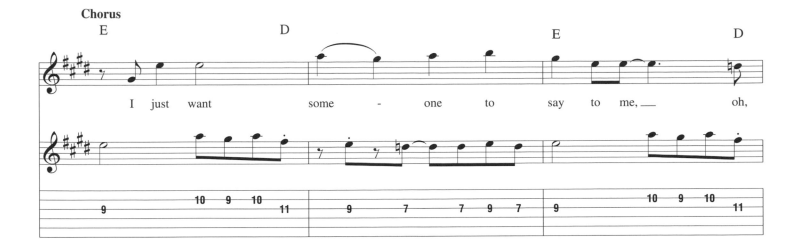

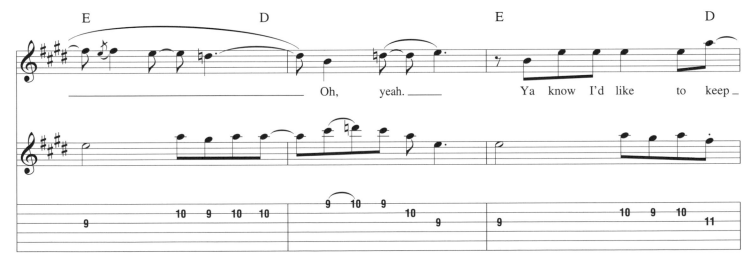

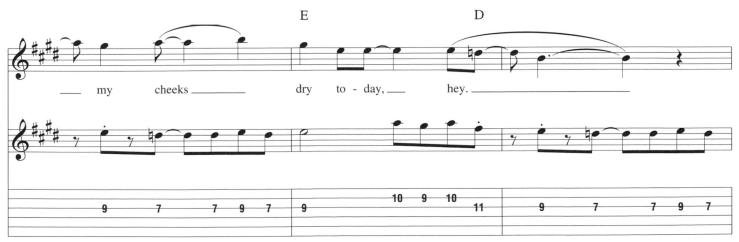

So stay with me ___ and I'll have it made. ___ Oh, oh, ___

Outro

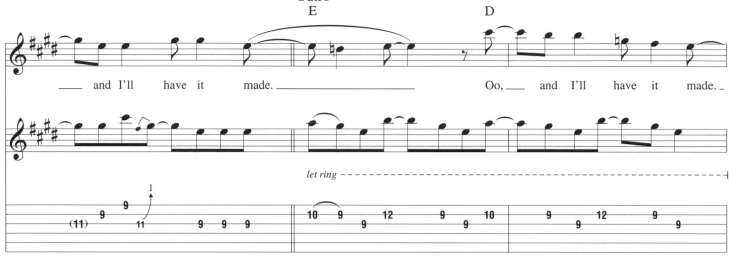

___ and I'll have it made. ___ Oo, ___ and I'll have it made. _

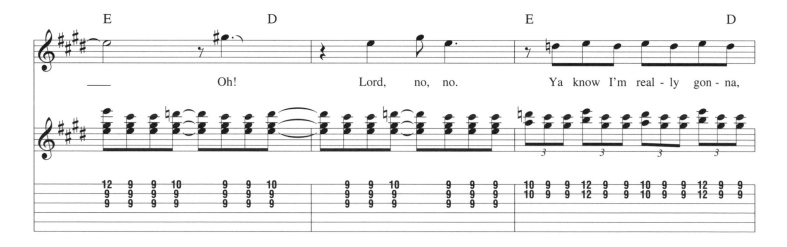

___ Oh! Lord, no, no. Ya know I'm real-ly gon-na,

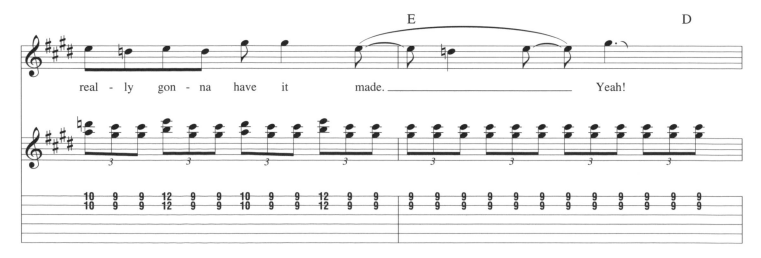

real-ly gon-na have it made. ___ Yeah!

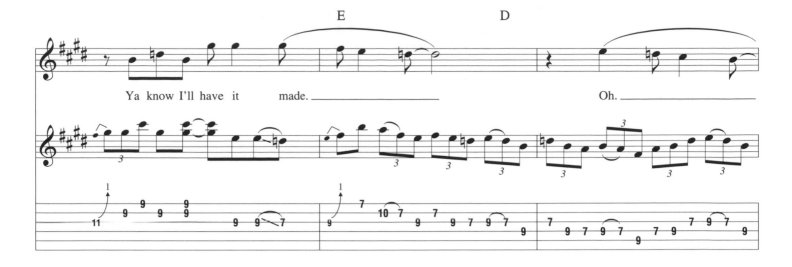

Ya know I'll have it made. _____ Oh. _____

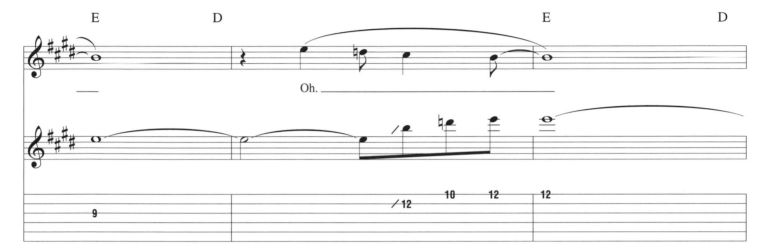

Oh. _____ Oh. _____

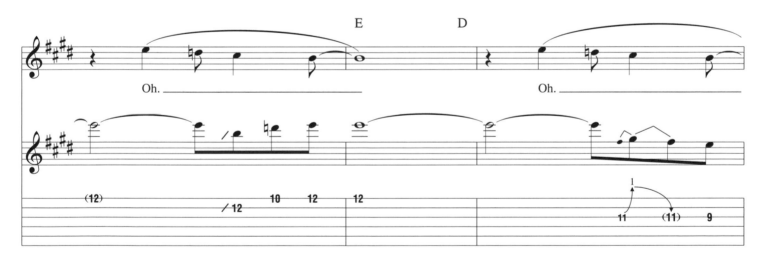

Oh. _____ Oh. _____

Oh, oh, oh, oh, oh. _____

Come as You Are

Words and Music by Kurt Cobain

Tune down one step:
(low to high) D-G-C-F-A-D

as a friend, __ as an old __ en - e - my. __

Take your time, __ hur - ry up, ____ the choice is yours, _

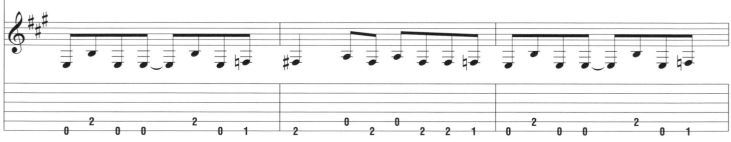

__ don't _ be late. ____ Take a rest ____ as a friend, _

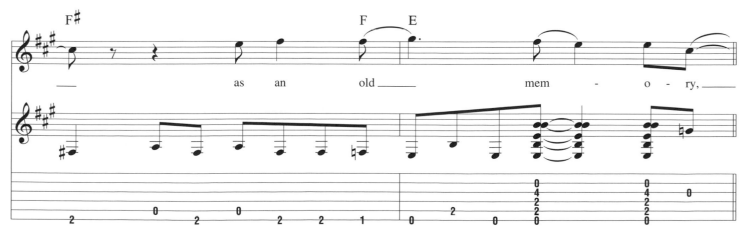

__ as an old _____ mem - o - ry, ____

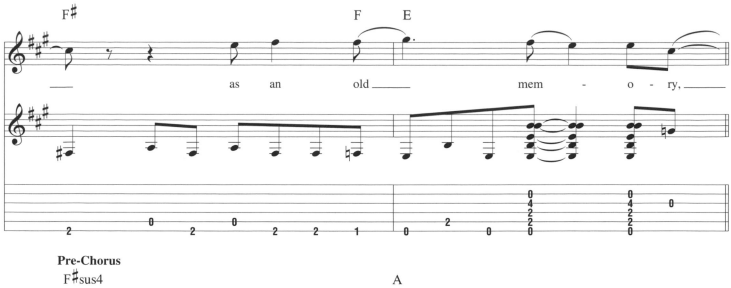

as an old_____ mem - o - ry,_____

Pre-Chorus

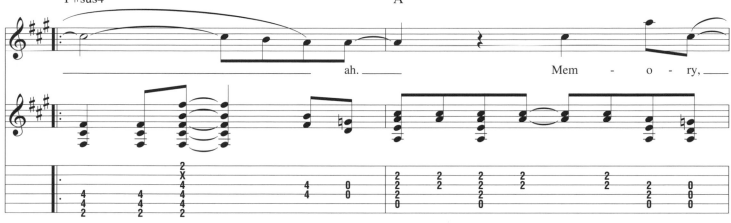

ah._____ Mem - o - ry,_____

ah._____ Mem - o - ry,_____

Chorus

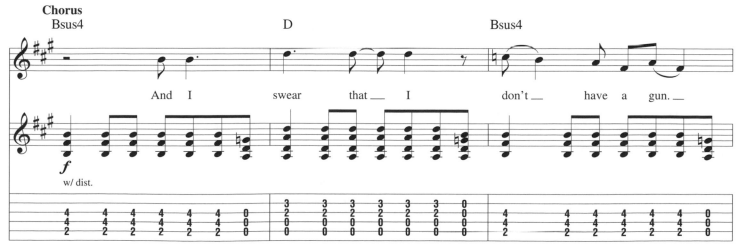

And I swear that___ I don't___ have a gun.___

No, I don't _____ have a gun. _____ No, I don't _____

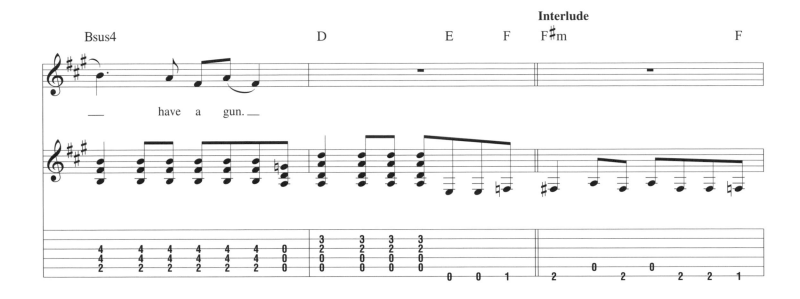

_____ have a gun. _____

Interlude

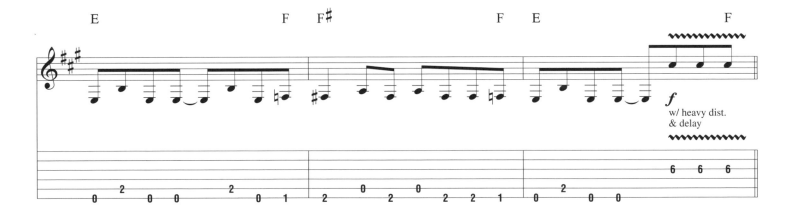

w/ heavy dist.
& delay

Guitar Solo

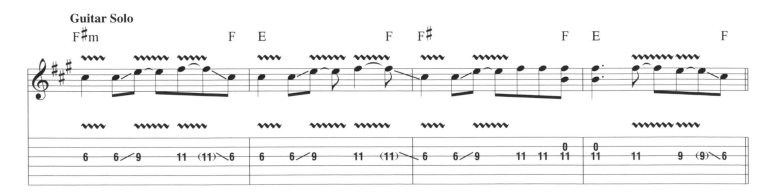

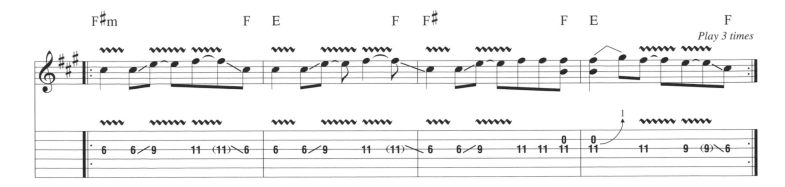

Pre-Chorus

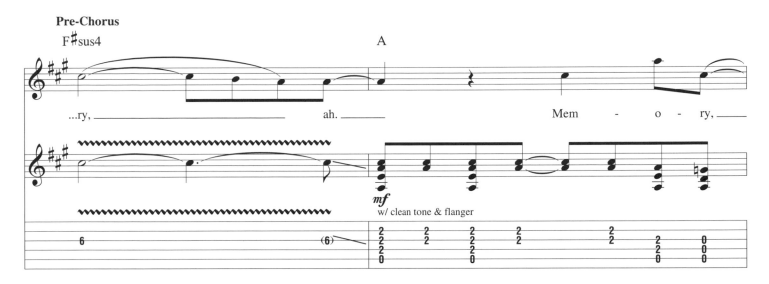

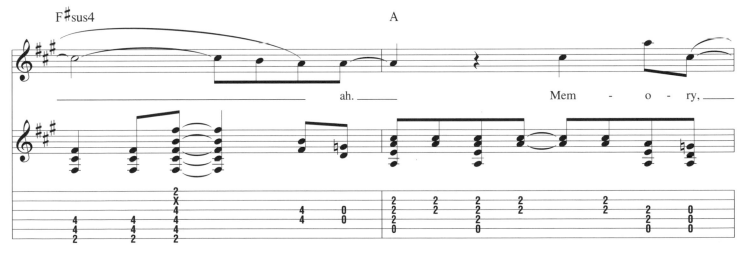

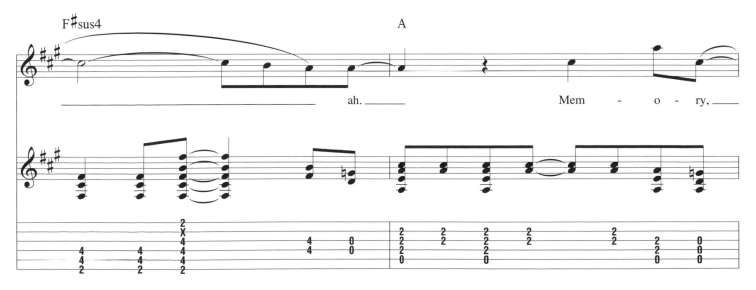

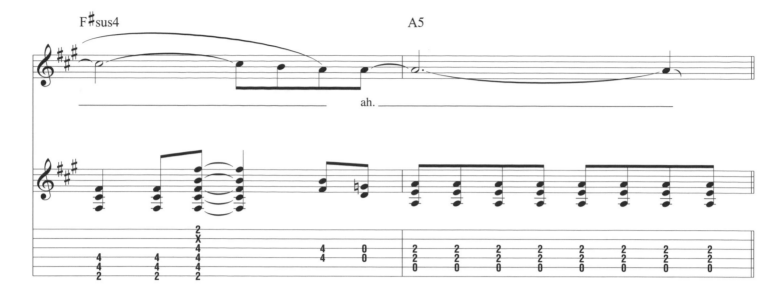

Chorus

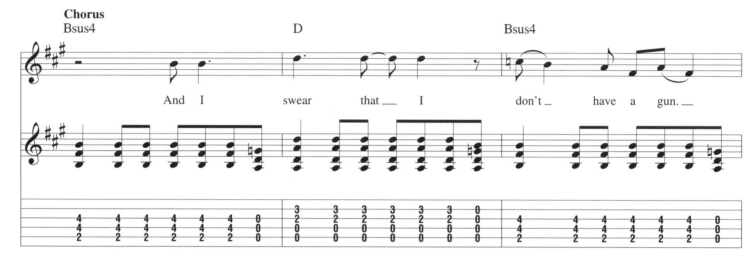

And I swear that I don't have a gun.

No, I don't have a gun. No, I don't

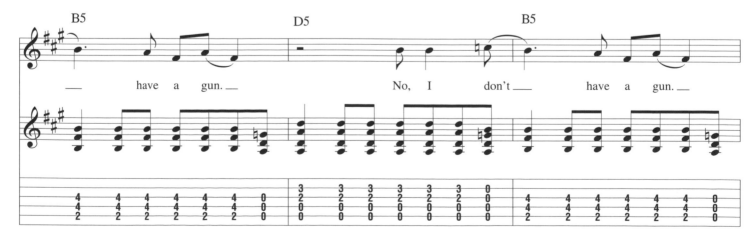

have a gun. No, I don't have a gun.

Give It Away

Written by Anthony Kiedis, Flea, John Frusciante and Chad Smith

Intro
Moderate Funk ♩ = 92
N.C.(A5)

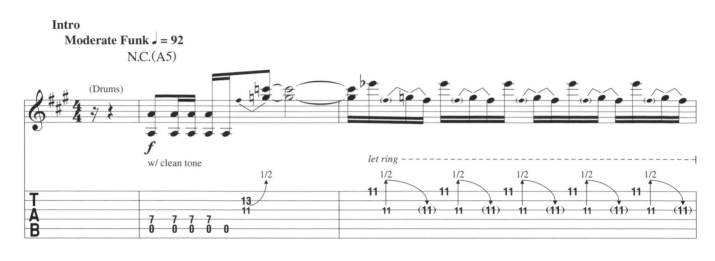

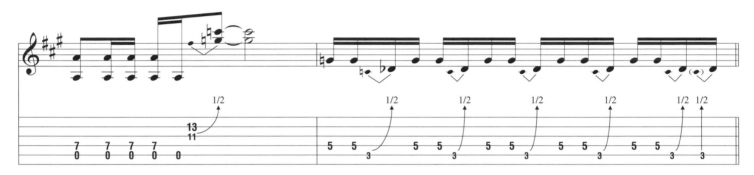

𝄋 Verse
N.C.(A5)

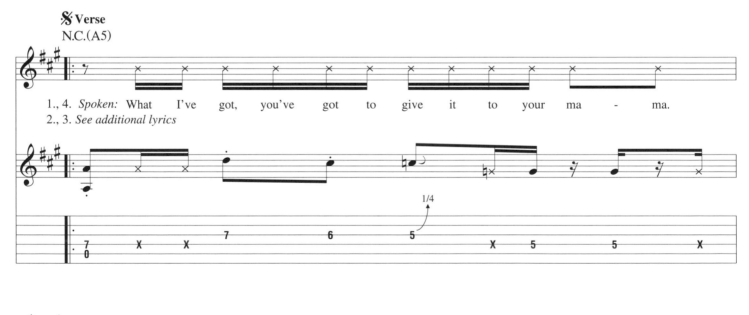

1., 4. *Spoken:* What I've got, you've got to give it to your ma - ma.
2., 3. *See additional lyrics*

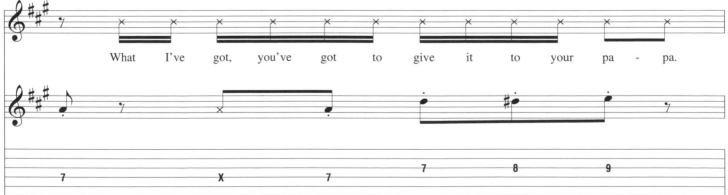

What I've got, you've got to give it to your pa - pa.

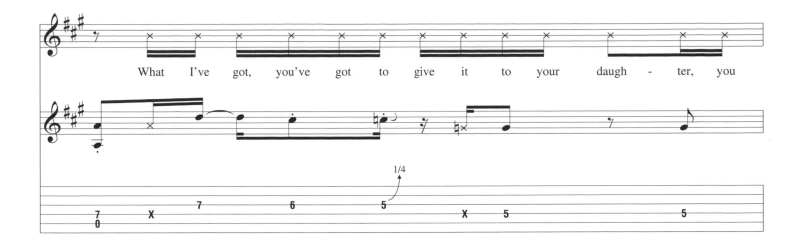

What I've got, you've got to give it to your daugh - ter, you

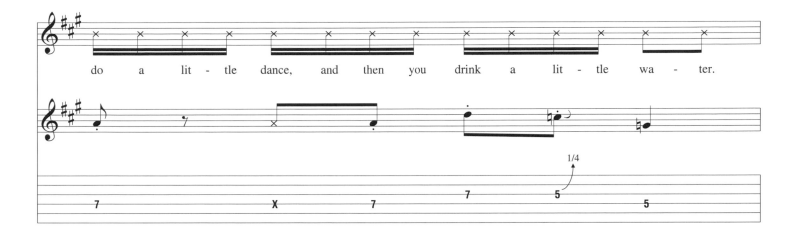

do a lit - tle dance, and then you drink a lit - tle wa - ter.

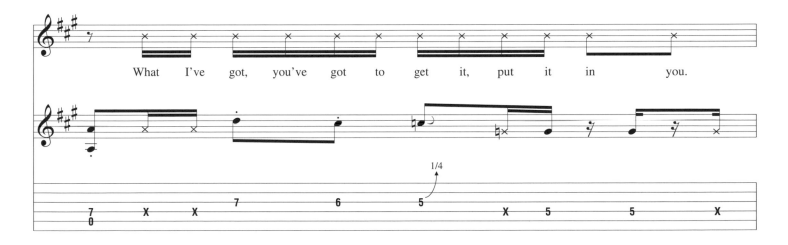

What I've got, you've got to get it, put it in you.

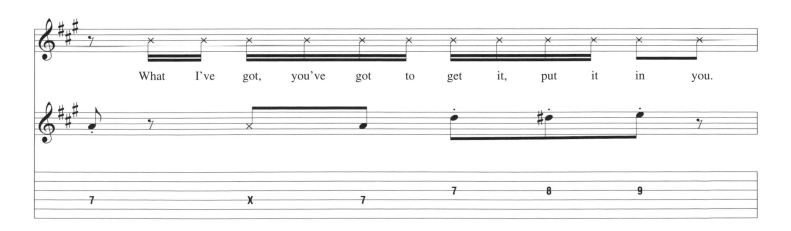

What I've got, you've got to get it, put it in you.

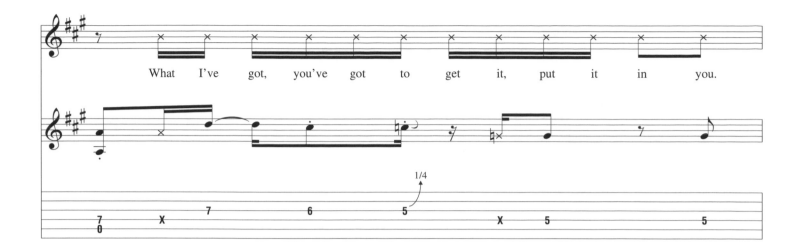

What I've got, you've got to get it, put it in you.

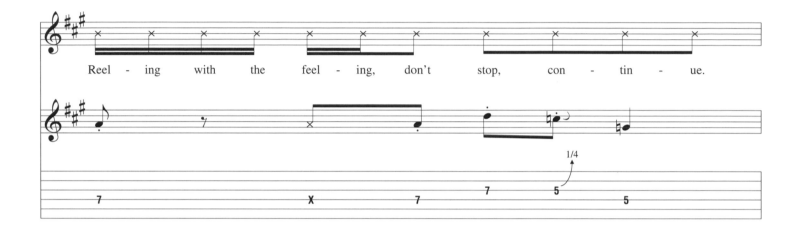

Reel - ing with the feel - ing, don't stop, con - tin - ue.

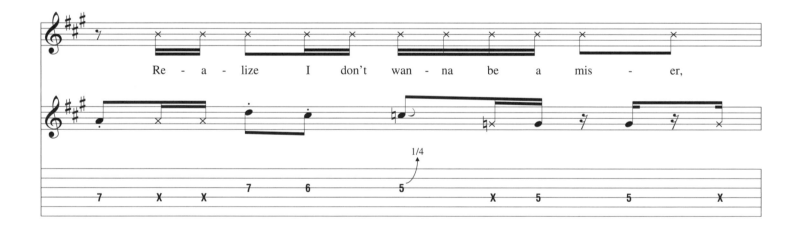

Re - a - lize I don't wan - na be a mis - er,

con - fide with Sly, you'll be the wis - er.

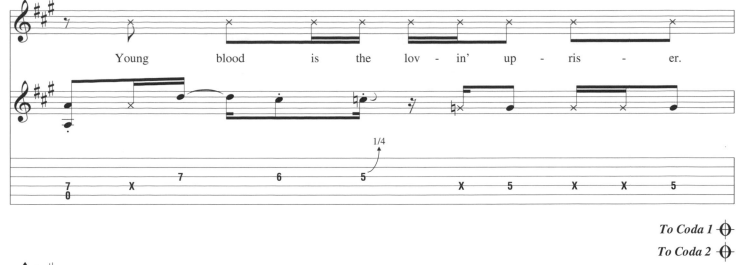

Young blood is the lov - in' up - ris - er.

To Coda 1 ⊕
To Coda 2 ⊕

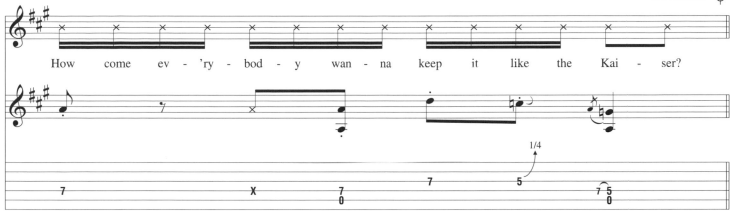

How come ev - 'ry - bod - y wan - na keep it like the Kai - ser?

Chorus

N.C.(A5)

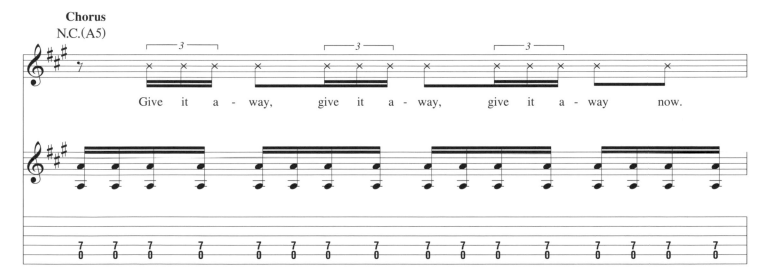

Give it a - way, give it a - way, give it a - way now.

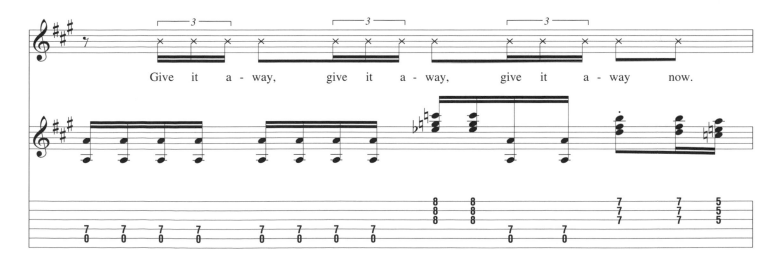

Give it a - way, give it a - way, give it a - way now.

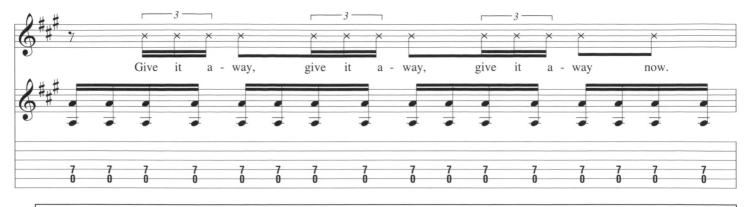

Give it a - way, give it a - way, give it a - way now.

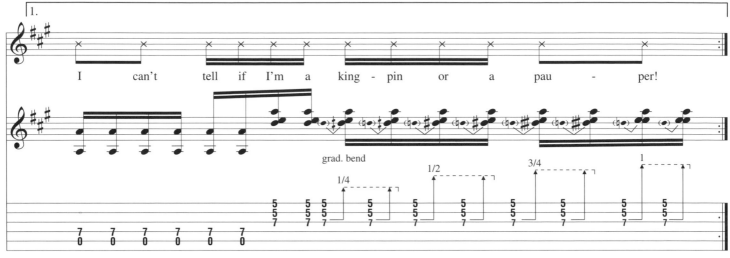

1.

I can't tell if I'm a king - pin or a pau - per!

grad. bend

2.

Oh, oh, yeah! ___

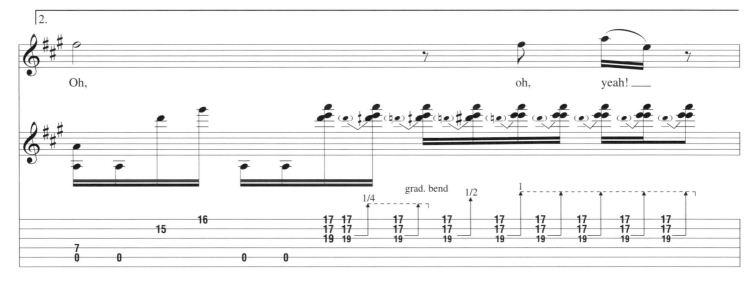

grad. bend

N.C.

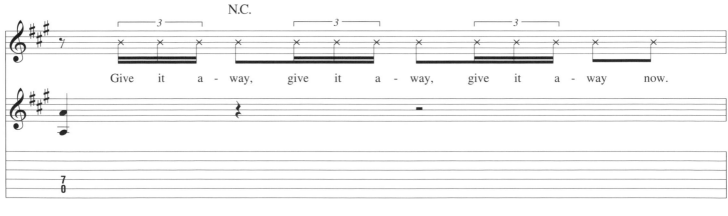

Give it a - way, give it a - way, give it a - way now.

Gtr. tacet

Give it a - way, give it a - way, give it a - way now. Give it a - way, give it a - way, give it a - way now.

Guitar Solo

N.C.(E5)

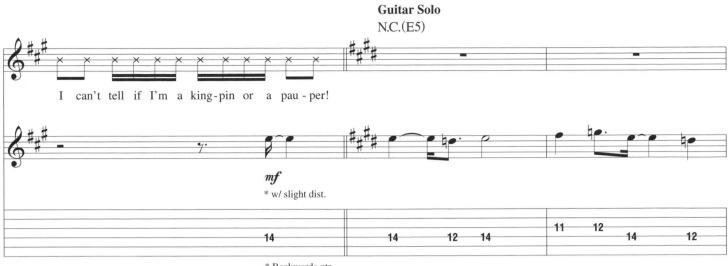

I can't tell if I'm a king-pin or a pau-per!

mf

* w/ slight dist.

* Backwards gtr.

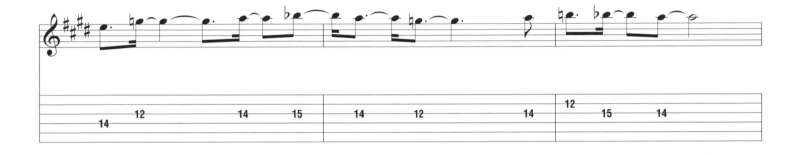

D.S. al Coda 1

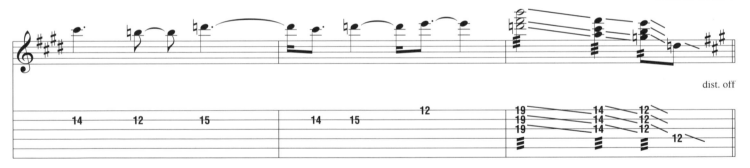

dist. off

Coda 1

N.C.

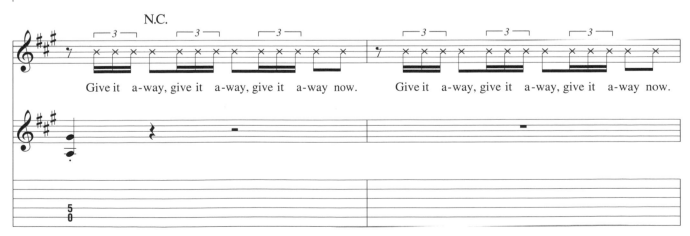

Give it a-way, give it a-way, give it a-way now.   Give it a-way, give it a-way, give it a-way now.

51

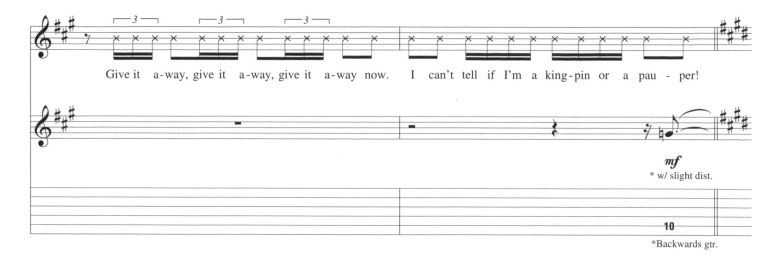

Give it a-way, give it a-way, give it a-way now. I can't tell if I'm a king-pin or a pau - per!

mf
* w/ slight dist.
*Backwards gtr.

Guitar Solo
N.C.(Em)

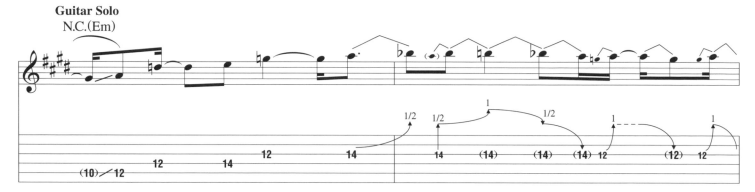

D.S. al Coda 2

dist. off

Coda 2

Outro-Chorus
N.C.(A5)

Give it a - way, give it a - way, give it a - way now.

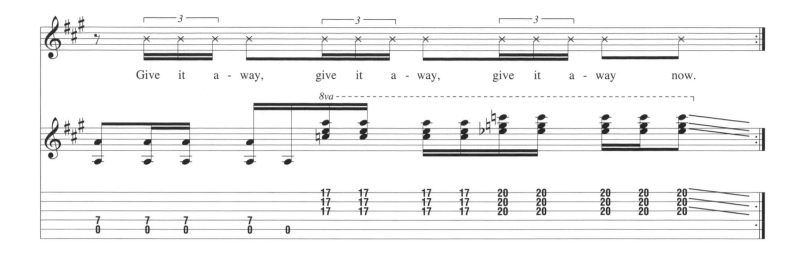

Give it a-way, give it a-way, give it a-way now.

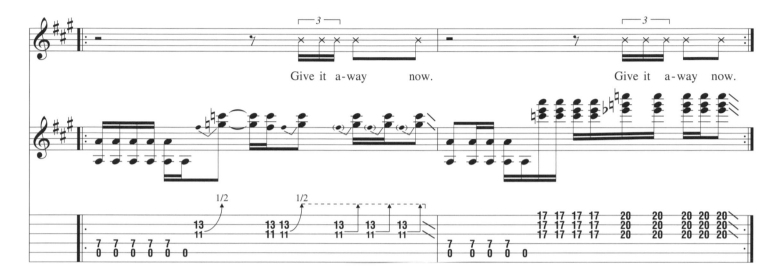

Give it a-way now. Give it a-way now.

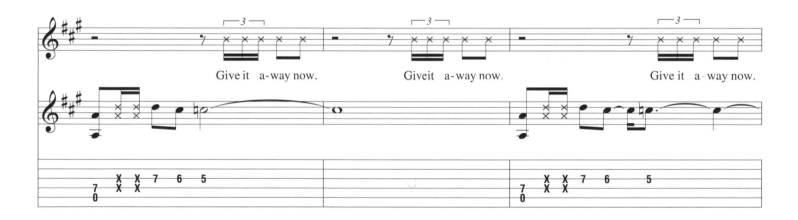

Give it a-way now. Give it a-way now. Give it a-way now.

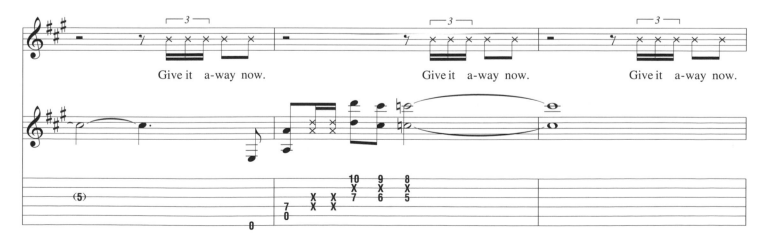

Give it a-way now. Give it a-way now. Give it a-way now.

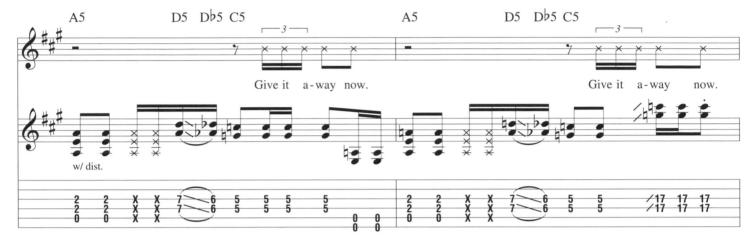

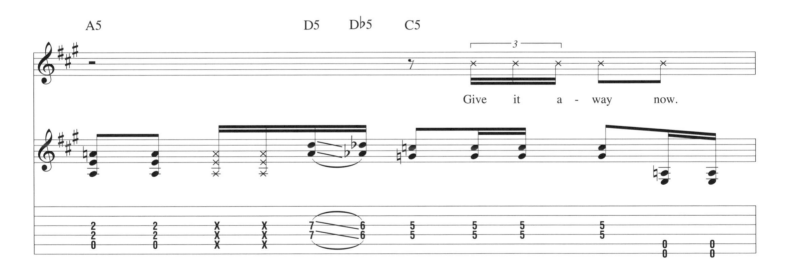

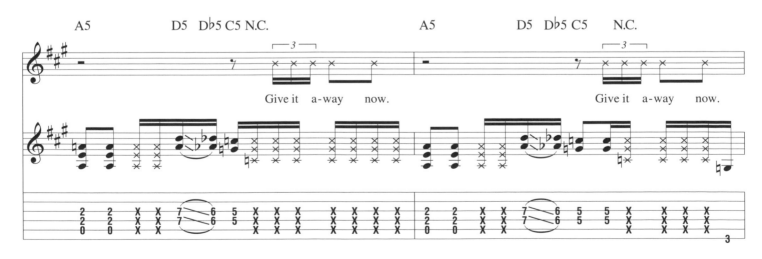

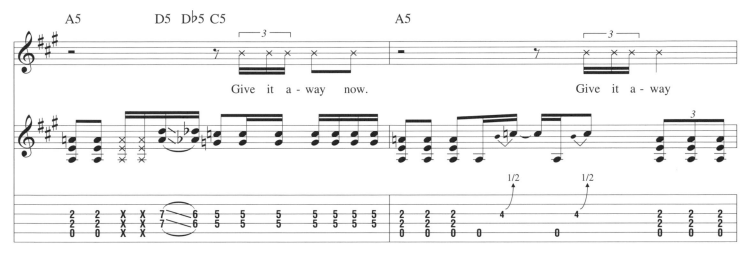

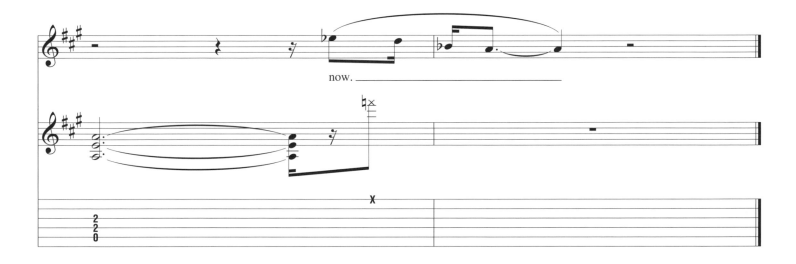

Additional Lyrics

2. Greedy little people in a sea of distress,
   Keep your move to receive your less.
   Unimpressed by material excess,
   Love is free, love me, say "Hell yes!"
   Low brow, but I rock a little know how.
   No time for the piggies or the hoosegow.
   Get smart, get down with the power,
   Never been a better time than right now.
   Bob Marley, poet and a prophet,
   Bob Marley taught me how to off it.
   Bob Marley walkin' like he talk it.
   Goodness me, can't you see I'm gonna cough it?

3. Lucky me, swimmin' in my ability,
   Dancin' down on life with agility.
   Come and drink it up from my fertility,
   Blessed with a bucket of lucky mobility.
   My mom, I love her 'cause she love me,
   Long gone are the times when she scrub me.
   Feelin' good, my brother gonna hug me,
   Drink up my juice, young love, chug-a-lug me.
   There's a river born to be a giver,
   Keep you warm, won't let you shiver.
   His heart is never gonna wither,
   Come on everybody, time to deliver.

No Excuses

Written by Jerry Cantrell

Tune down 1/2 step:
(low to high) E♭-A♭-D♭-G♭-B♭-E♭

Intro
Moderately ♩ = 114

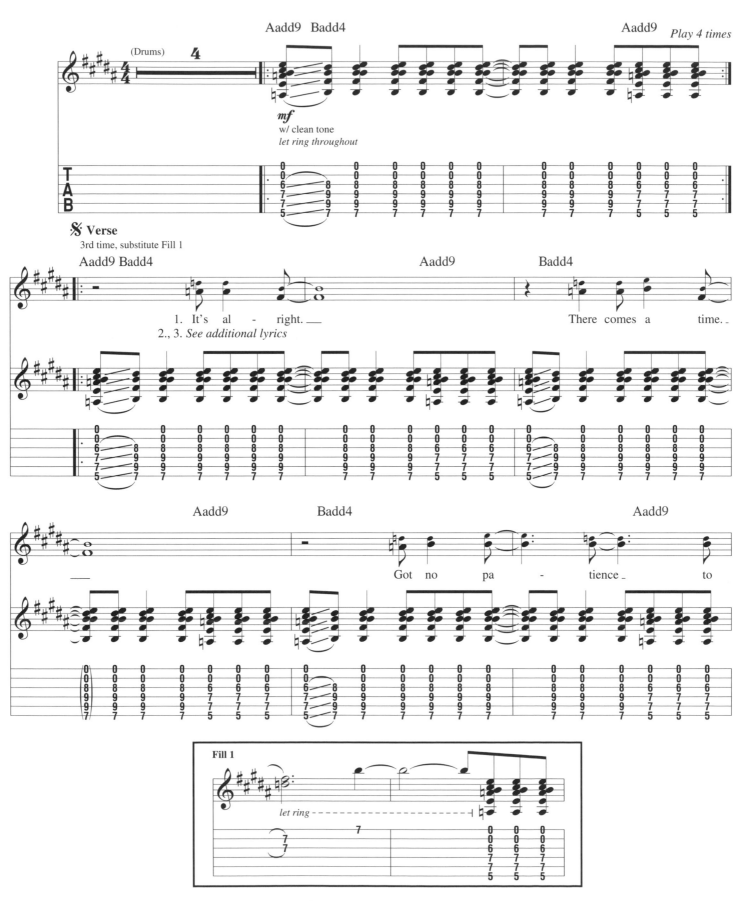

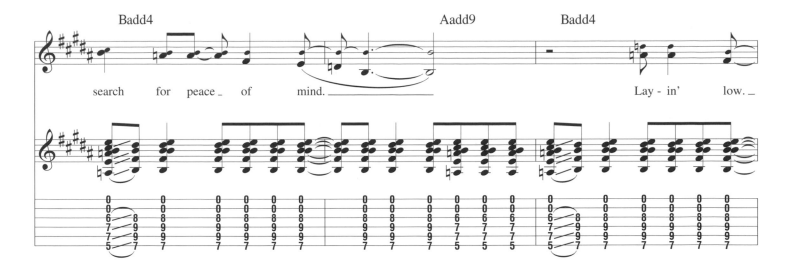

search for peace _ of mind. _____ Lay - in' low. _

_ Want to take it slow. __

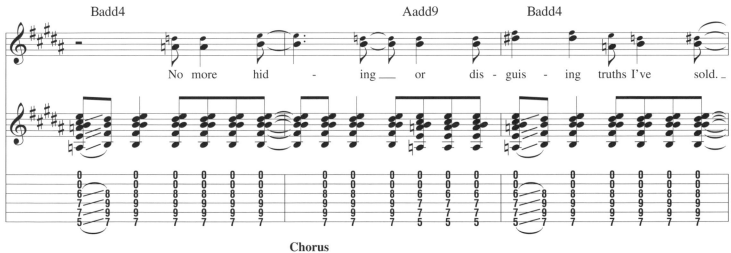

No more hid - ing ___ or dis - guis - ing truths I've sold. _

Chorus

Ev - 'ry - day ___ it's some - thing, hits _

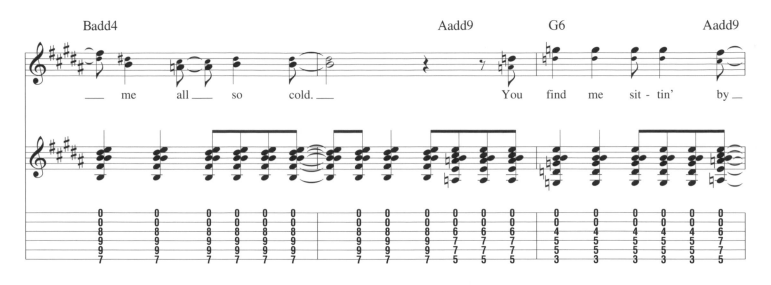

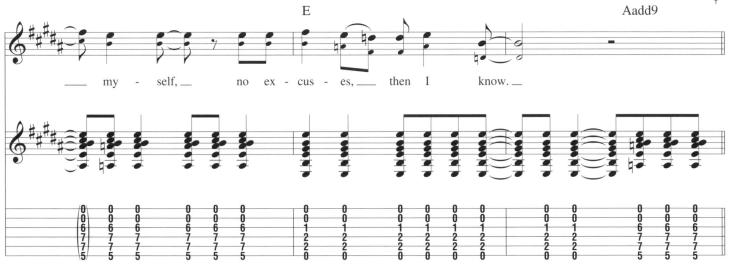

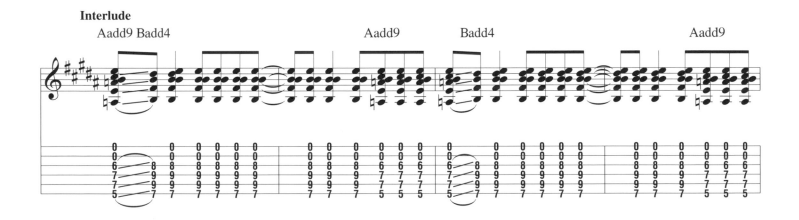

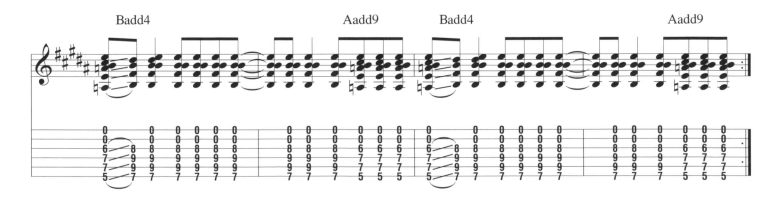

Guitar Solo

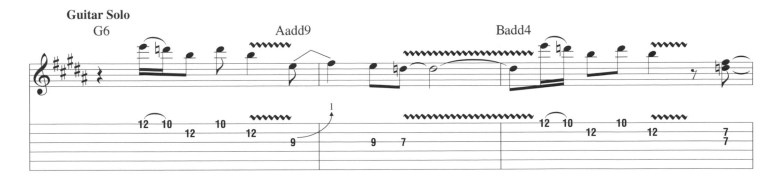

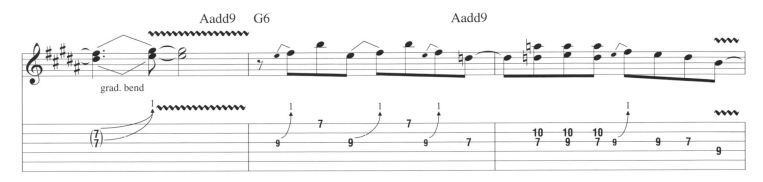

D.S. al Coda

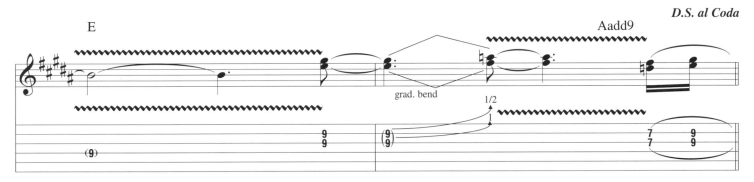

Coda

Outro

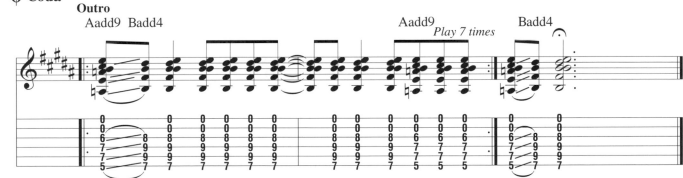

Additional Lyrics

2. It's okay. Had a bad day.
   Hands are bruised from breaking rocks all day.
   Drained and blue, I bleed for you.
   You think it's funny, well, you're drowning in it too.

3. Yeah, it's fine. We'll walk down the line.
   Leave our rain, a cold trade for warm sunshine.
   You, my friend, I will defend.
   And if we change, well, I love you anyway.

Santeria

Words and Music by Brad Nowell, Eric Wilson and Floyd Gaugh

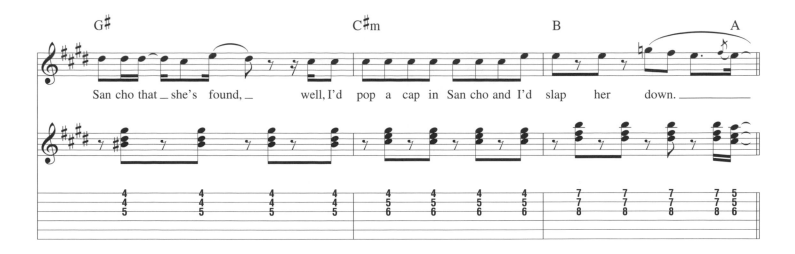

San cho that _ she's found, _ well, I'd pop a cap in San cho and I'd slap her down. _____

Chorus

_ What I real-ly wan-na know, _ my ba- by, mm. _____ What I real-ly wan-na say _

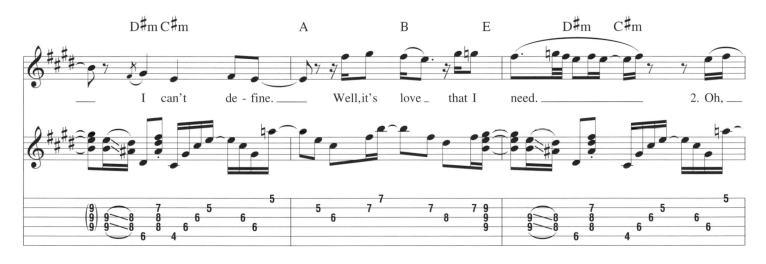

_ I can't de - fine. _____ Well, it's love _ that I need. _____ 2. Oh, _

𝄉 Verse

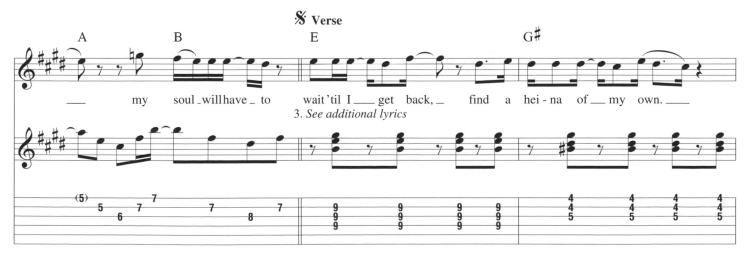

_ my soul _ will have _ to wait 'til I ____ get back, _ find a hei - na of __ my own. _____
3. *See additional lyrics*

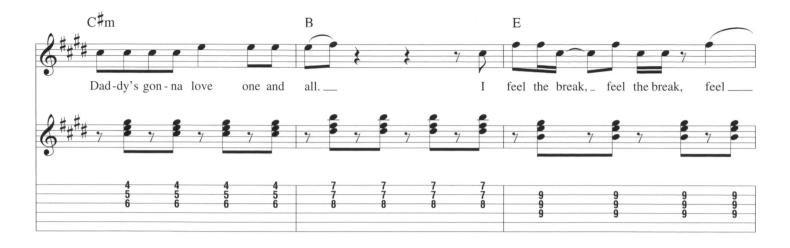

Chorus

See additional lyrics

To Coda ⊕

Guitar Solo

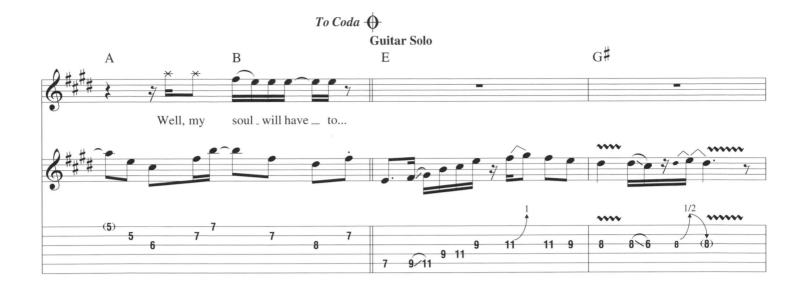

Well, my soul will have to...

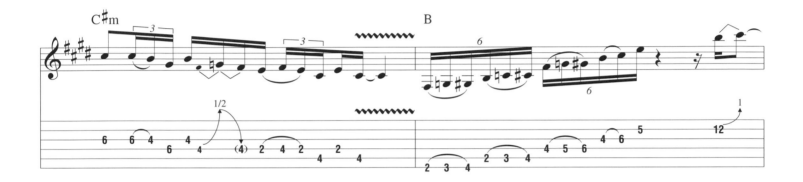

Chorus

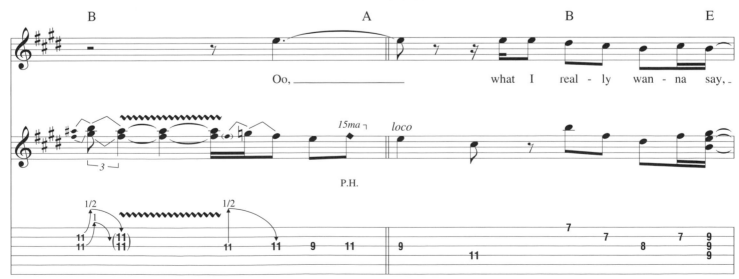

Oo, _____ what I real - ly wan - na say, __

P.H.

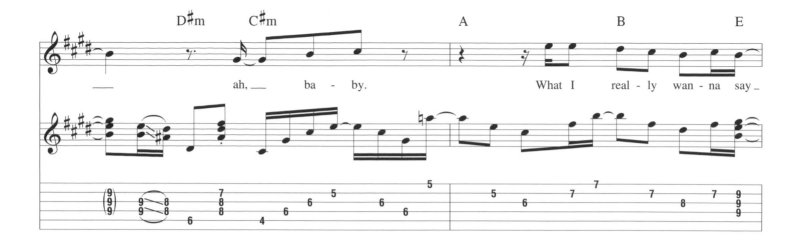

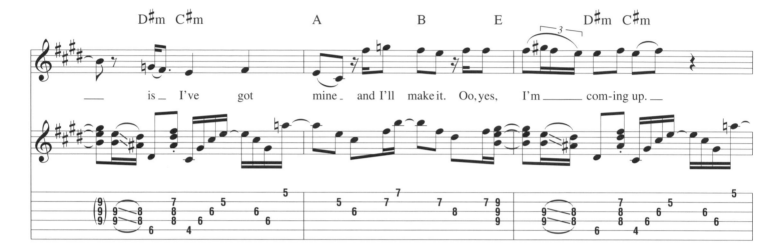

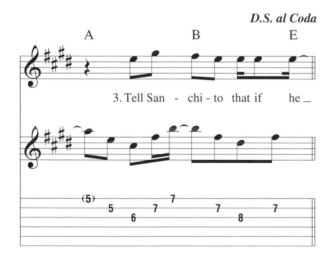

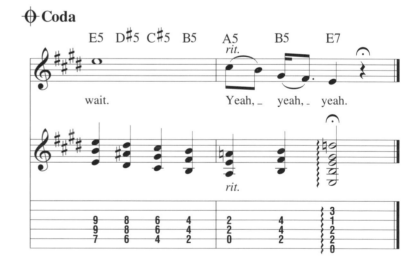

Additional Lyrics

3. Tell Sanchito that if he knows what is good for him
   He best go run and hide.
   Daddy's got a new .45
   And I won't think twice to stick that barrel
   Straight down Sancho's throat.
   Believe me when I say that I
   Got something for his punk ass.

Chorus What I really wanna know, my baby.
   Oo, what I really wanna say is there's just
   One way back and I'll make it.
   Yeah, my soul will have to wait. Yeah, yeah, yeah.